THE
HOLOCAUST
DIARIES

כָּל זֹאת בָּאַתְנוּ וְלֹא שְׁכַחֲנוּךָ
(תהלים מד:יח)

All this has befallen us
yet we have not forgotten You
(*Tehillim* 44:18)

# Sisters in the Storm

The Holocaust Diaries

# Sisters in the Storm

## Anna Eilenberg

CIS

P·U·B·L·I·S·H·E·R·S

New York · London · Jerusalem

Published and distributed
in the U.S., Canada and overseas by
C.I.S. Publishers and Distributors
180 Park Avenue, Lakewood, New Jersey 08701
(908) 905-3000 Fax: (908) 367-6666

Distributed in Israel by
C.I.S. International (Israel)
Rechov Mishkalov 18
Har Nof, Jerusalem
Tel: 02-518-935

Distributed in the U.K. and Europe by
C.I.S. International (U.K.)
89 Craven Park Road
London N15 6AH, England
Tel: 81-809-3723

Book and cover design: Deenee Cohen
Typography: Nechamie Miller

Cover illustration reproduced
from original painting by Francis McGinley

ISBN 1-56062-156-7
Library of Congress Catalog Card Number
92-082715

PRINTED IN THE UNITED STATES OF AMERICA

ספר זה מוקדש
לזכר נשמת


אבי מורי
ראובן יוסף בן אלחנן אהרן הי"ד


אמי מורתי
אסתר איטה בת יחיאל הי"ד


אחי
אברהם בנימין בן ראובן יוסף הי"ד


שנהרגו על קידוש השם בגטו לדז'


ת.נ.צ.ב.ה.

# TABLE OF CONTENTS

—————————————■—————————————

Publisher's Note ............................................................... 15

## BOOK ONE

### The Storm Approaches

1. This Place Called Home ............................................. 23
2. Bnos Agudas Yisrael ................................................. 29
3. Summer Strike ........................................................... 36
4. Bird Food .................................................................... 40
5. Rude Awakenings ...................................................... 45

## BOOK TWO

### The Storm Breaks

6. Visits to the Hospital ................................................ 55
7. The Walls Close In ..................................................... 60

8. A Place to Live .......................................................... 68
9. Defiance of Death ...................................................... 73
10. The Relief List .......................................................... 79
11. Warring Over Wood .................................................. 86
12. Not the Children! ...................................................... 93
13. Five Small Potatoes .................................................. 99
14. Slipping Sanity ........................................................ 109
15. Disintegration of a Family .................................... 117

## BOOK THREE

### The Fury of the Storm

16. The Mice Are Caught .............................................. 127
17. Welcome to Auschwitz ............................................ 134
18. The Endless Nightmare .......................................... 143
19. Diversions ................................................................ 152
20. Tefillos and Tefillin ................................................ 162
21. A Journey to the Left .............................................. 166
22. A Moment of Weakness .......................................... 173
23. Slave Trade .............................................................. 177

## BOOK FOUR

### The Ravages of the Storm

24. The End of Winter .................................................. 189
25. The Peasant Woman ................................................ 194
26. Searching for Father .............................................. 198
27. The Journey Home .................................................. 203
28. Lodgings .................................................................. 211
29. Out of Poland ........................................................ 223
30. Trouble with Trains ................................................ 228
31. Russian Roulette .................................................... 236

# BOOK FIVE

## The Aftermath of the Storm

32. A Question of Directions ......................................... 245
33. A Dreadful Disappointment................................... 252
34. The Real Thing .......................................................... 257
35. Marking Time in Zagreb .................................... 261
36. The Sea Voyage Begins .................................... 269
37. Encounters with the British .................................. 276
38. Settling In.............................................................. 283
39. Matchmaking .......................................................... 292
40. So Near, Yet So Far .................................................. 299

Epilogue ........................................................................ 309
Pictorial Section .......................................................... 311
Glossary ........................................................................ 315

# PUBLISHER'S NOTE

—————————■—————————

I MMEDIATELY AFTER THEIR LIGHTNING CONQUEST OF Poland, the Germans launched their genocidal assault against the millions of frightened and defenseless Jews in the captive territories. The assault began with confiscations, restrictive edicts, harassment and random violence, but it quickly moved into a more diabolical stage of the Nazi systematic master plan to obliterate the Jews. The Jews were isolated in numerous congested and heavily guarded ghettoes where they were exploited as slave laborers while they awaited their sinister fate.

The everyday struggle for survival in the ghetto was brutal. Food and fuel were in critically short supply. Epidemic diseases caused by unsanitary conditions raged through the impossibly overcrowded buildings. The expired bodies of emaciated ghetto dwellers littered the streets, and the stench of death was everywhere. Then began the *Aktionen*, the terrifying roundups of those not felled by hunger, exposure or disease for deportation to the newly operational extermination camps. At the first signs of an impending *Aktion*, many people fled into specially constructed hideouts known as "bunkers," but more often than not, they were discovered by the Nazi searchers and their snarling bloodhounds, if not in this *Aktion* then in the next one or the one after that. Ultimately, the ghettoes were liquidated, with only a pitifully small remnant of survivors managing to escape the bloody dragnets. *Sisters in the Storm* tells the all too typical story of a sheltered teenage girl who lived through the miseries and heartbreak of the ghetto and was eventually deported to Auschwitz.

*Sisters in the Storm* begins with a description of Lodz, Poland, during the last years of evanescent peace when the author was little more than a child. It was a time when the innocence of youth still bloomed, a time enriched by the warmth and intense spirituality of family life even if material possessions were lacking, a time when the sounds of Torah and *tefillah* and animated conversation reverberated through the teeming Jewish streets of Lodz, one of the largest and most vibrant Jewish communities of pre-War Europe. The author also provides a very valuable description of the powerful influence of the educational *Shabbos* programs of Bnos Agudas Yisrael on the young Jewish girls of Poland before the war, especially those who could not afford to attend one of the new Bais Yaakov schools; some of the author's fondest pre-War memories are of the warmth, encouragement and companionship provided by Bnos. All in all, for the author's family, as for most of the Jews of Lodz, life

16

before the war was a constant struggle against poverty, but it was nevertheless filled with happiness and profound fulfillment. And then the Nazi juggernaut struck like a malevolent thunderbolt out of a hellish sky, instantly destroying a world that had taken centuries to build and reducing its inhabitants to a degraded, bestial level of existence.

The Lodz ghetto was the largest in Poland, except for the Warsaw ghetto, but whereas the Warsaw ghetto perished in the flames of a thoroughly one-sided battle, the Lodz ghetto was liquidated by deportations, as were the other ghettoes of Poland. Because of the sheer size of its population, however, and the minuscule area allotted to it, conditions in the Lodz ghetto were more appalling than virtually anywhere else. Thus, in little more than the blinking of an eye, the idyllic and roseate hues of the author's sheltered childhood exploded into a maelstrom of shock, violence, confusion and unbearable desperation. And she responded with bravery, courage and resourcefulness remarkable for a girl in her early teens. When the first Germans appeared on the streets of Lodz, she volunteered to forage for food so that her bearded father and brother could remain out of sight, and when the ghetto walls were erected, she and her sister became the principal breadwinners of the family. But the destruction of her family and her subsequent deportation to Auschwitz snuffed out the bright sparks of youthful spirit, replacing them with a gnawing sense of despair and a dogged, almost mechanical determination to survive.

By the time the author and her sister were deported to Auschwitz, they were the only remnants of her family, and they clung to each other with the fierce devotion and selfless sacrifice characteristic of numerous other siblings and close relatives and friends who endured the nightmare together. In this darkest hour, with the specter of death a ubiquitous companion, the instinct for self-preservation was transcended by the finer instincts of humanity, and concern for a sibling, a parent, a child or a close friend became more important than survival itself. This intense, self-negating devotion to loved ones may also have reflected a desperate desire to hold on to the last vestiges of vanished times; when all else had been destroyed, only these personal relationships remained as a tenuous connection to the past.

One of the more remarkable, heroic images that emerges from this book is the author's loving portrait of her older brother, a *chassidic* young man who refused to compromise the purity of his soul, fervent devotion to Torah study and the sheer joy of Jewish observance, no matter the personal costs. In the most difficult times in the ghetto, his saintliness, integrity and clarity of thought helped her find a semblance of balance in a world gone utterly mad. And during her further tribulations, when her brother had already surrendered his unsullied soul to its Maker, his memory remained an indelible source of solace and inspiration.

As the book nears its conclusion in the immediate aftermath of the war, when the broken and disoriented survivors tried to recapture a modicum of normalcy, we once again find a revitalized Bnos Agudas Yisrael playing a major role in the healing and rebuilding process, a veritable bulwark of strength and stability for a whole generation of young women torn away from an authentic Jewish existence during their formative years. The dedicated leaders of Bnos took the place of the girls' absent parents, providing them with care and love and nurturing their precious memories of the pure Yiddishkeit of their early lives until they blossomed into wonderful young Jewish women of whom their parents would have been proud, young women who would build a shining new Jewish world on the deeply mourned ashes of the old.

The final part of the book offers a fascinating firsthand account of the experiences of those survivors who chose to emigrate to Palestine, including encounters with the British Navy on the high seas and internment in displaced persons camps in Cyprus.

*Sisters in the Storm* is a story that is remarkable in its typicality, a highly readable story that provides deep insight into the thoughts and feelings of all those who passed through the inhuman crucible of German fiendishness, of those who perished and those who survived.

Three years ago, C.I.S. Publishers launched the *Holocaust Diaries* collection with the publication of *Late Shadows* by Moshe Holczler. At that time, our goal was to assemble an organized body of holocaust literature written from the Orthodox perspective, a unified body of literature that would stand as an everlasting testament to the invincibility of the Jewish spirit nurtured on Torah, *mitzvos* and unstinting devotion to the *Ribono Shel Olam*. We decided to limit inclusion in the *Holocaust Diaries* to distinguished autobiographical accounts by survivors, with as wide a variation of experience and locale as possible. We also decided to present these memoirs as a collective unit so that they would endure as a valuable resource for future generations and not fall by the wayside with the passage of time.

With the publication of *Sisters in the Storm*, the *Holocaust Diaries* collection has grown to five published volumes, each an important work in its own right. *Late Shadows* by Moshe Holczler describes the experiences of Hungarian Jewry under Nazi occupation as well as numerous reports of other survivors. *They Called Me Frau Anna* by Chana Marcus Banet is the story of a mother and her children who survive the war on falsified Aryan papers. *Dare to Survive* by Chaim Shlomo Friedman is a story of faith and daring in the ghettoes of Cracow, Bochnia and Tarnow. *Behind the Ice Curtain* by Dina Gabel describes the experiences of the refugees and deportees who spent the war years in Siberia. As for the future, a number of volumes of similar stature are in preparation or under consideration. Thus, in three short years, the dream has become a reality, and we would like to offer a prayer of gratitude to the *Ribono Shel Olam* for blessing our efforts with such gratifying success and a prayer of supplication that He continue to look with favor upon our future efforts in this and other projects that bring honor to His Name.

At this time, we would like to take the opportunity to acknowledge the contributions of all those who have helped bring the dream to fruition: Editorial Director Raizy Kaufman, whose adroit and sensitive guidance has been the driving force of this project from its inception through each individual volume; Staff Editor Pnina Soloveitchik, the editor of this book, whose superb skills are reflected in its final form; Art Director Deenee Cohen, whose stellar artistic talents enhance every project she touches; Typographer Nechamie Miller, whose technical skills and efficiency are manifest in the production; and all the other members of our splendid staff who strive to make each book a jewel unto itself. May the *Ribono Shel Olam* reward them generously for their devoted efforts, and may we all continue to work together productively and in harmony for many years to come.

Y.Y.R.
Lakewood, N.J.
*Menachem Av*, 5752 (1992)

BOOK ONE

———————■———————

The
Storm
Approaches

# CHAPTER 1

■

# This Place Called Home

W HEN I CAST MY MIND BACK TO MY CHILDHOOD, I visualize my grandparents' apartment in Lodz, Poland. I was born there, and we stayed in the apartment until I was nine years old. It had only two rooms, a bedroom and a large kitchen, but it was home.

The apartment was on the third floor at 18 Wolborska Street, right across the street from the Alteshtetishe Shul, the most magnificent *shul* in Lodz. The bedroom had two small windows facing the *shul*. The kitchen had one large window facing the courtyard of the *beis medrash*, where my grandfather had a *Mishnayos chaburah* that began at four in the morning.

Our share of the apartment was the bedroom; we stayed in that one room all the time. It was on the third floor, with a slanted ceiling, no plumbing and no running water. All these things didn't really matter, though; it was home, a place of warmth and love that outshone any flaws or problems that might have existed.

Friday afternoons were a wonderful mixture of chaos and organization. The floor was scrubbed to a shine and sprinkled with golden sand. The table was bedecked with the pure white linen tablecloth, and the crystal bottle was filled with sparkling wine. The freshly baked *challos*, with their tempting aroma, lay beneath a lovely velvet cloth. Everyone was busy, rushing to wash, dress and take care of all the last-minute things so that we would be ready to welcome *Shabbos* into our home.

I had my own special ritual for *Shabbos* mornings. I used to sit by the window, with my nose pressed against the glass, waiting to see my mother and grandmother walk down the wide, shining steps of the *shul* after *Shacharis*. I would get more and more excited as they walked across the street among the other women. I was sure that nobody got dressed for *Shabbos* as nicely as they did. Then, mentally counting the number of steps they had to walk up once they entered the building, I was ready to throw myself into their arms the moment they walked into the apartment.

I'm surprised at how vivid these memories are in my mind today. I feel as if I could reach out and touch the nuts with which we played, or hug my grandfather as he sat on the floor with us and played games, or stand quietly as I look over my father's shoulder to watch him do his work as a *sofer*.

I loved the stories my grandmother used to tell us. One story she used to tell us began with "once upon a time," even though we all knew it was a true story that had taken place very recently.

The story went as follows: Once upon a time, a well-to-do merchant came to Lodz to find a *shidduch* for his daughter. He was interested in a boy who was a *talmid chacham* and a *baal midos*. The merchant came to the Wilke Shul to ask the *gabbai* of the *shul* for advice. The *gabbai* pointed to a young man sitting in the corner. He told the merchant that this boy was the greatest *masmid* he had ever seen and would be the perfect match for his daughter.

The merchant spent a few days watching the *bachur*, and he became more and more impressed with him with each passing hour. When the boy's father came to the *shul* with food for his son, the merchant introduced himself and started a conversation with the father.

The *bachur's* father looked fondly at his son, sitting in his corner, completely oblivious to everything around him. "If I would not bring him a bit of rice or a potato," he said, "my son would not come home to eat, even though we live right next door. This boy of mine cares about nothing but learning."

The merchant liked this and wanted to know more. The father of the boy invited the merchant to his home, and they discussed the *shidduch*. They agreed that the merchant would support the young couple so that the boy would be able to learn without worrying about a *parnassah* for the first years of his marriage. They drank a *lechayim*, wished each other *mazel tov*, and their children were engaged. The merchant went home to inform his wife and daughter that there would soon be a wedding, and the *bachur* found out he was a *chassan* when he came home that night at midnight from *shul*.

My grandmother always ended the story there, but there would be a big smile on her face. She knew that we knew that she was telling us the story of how Tatteshe and Mammeshe had become engaged.

My mother also used to tell us stories, keeping us fascinated for hours on end. One of the stories my mother loved telling us was about the time the Gerrer Rebbe came to Wloclawek, where my parents lived when they were first married. When he passed the street where my parents were living, he stopped. The sweet sounds of my father learning *Gemara* were clearly audible, and the enthusiasm and *hasmadah* in my father's voice caught the Rebbe's attention. He asked the people with him if they knew who was learning with such fervor.

One of the Rebbe's escorts knocked on my father's door and asked him to come down and meet the Rebbe. My father, both surprised and elated, spoke with the Gerrer Rebbe. My mother, however, was even more excited. The idea that her husband had been *zocheh* to catch the Gerrer Rebbe's attention was an honor she had never dreamed of. She used to tell and retell the story, speaking proudly about our father and his great *hasmadah* in learning. I think she told us the story so often because she wanted to give us something to which to aspire.

Tatteshe became a *sofer* when he needed to find a *parnassah.* I was always so proud that so many Gerrer *chassidim* were eager to have a *Sefer Torah* written by my father. His clients kept him very busy writing *mezuzos, tefillin parshiyos* and *Sifrei Torah.* I loved to watch him, and I had learned from a very young age to be absolutely quiet when Tatteshe was working.

It was fascinating to watch how much concentration and *yiras shamayim* went into every letter he put down on the parchment. He was so careful to make sure that he had the right *machshavos* in mind with every stroke of his quill. Tatteshe was always slightly behind in his work, because he put so much effort into all the *tashmishei kedushah* he wrote.

Everyone always assured him, though, that the wait was well worth it. Even today, there is a man in *Eretz Yisrael* who owns a pair of *tefillin* with *parshiyos* written by my father. We asked him to sell it to us, but he refused. He told us that the *tefillin* were one of the most valuable things he owned.

My parents' major concern was always to ensure that we children had good *midos*, good *hashkafos* and the right priorities in life. They were always so patient with us. If one of us demanded to know why we couldn't draw a picture on *Shabbos*, or asked why we had to follow a *halachah* that didn't make sense to us, my father would calmly sit the child down at the table. Pulling out a *Chumash*, a *Shulchan Aruch* or another *sefer*, he would sit down with the child and learn the *halachah*, patiently explaining the reasoning behind it.

Tatteshe always found time to learn with us. I was still very young when my father taught me *Mesilas Yesharim* in Hebrew. He also read to us from *sefarim* written by Rav Shamshon Refael Hirsch, in the original German. He listened to all my problems, no matter how trivial; to me, they were of earth-shaking importance, and my father understood.

Mammeshe taught us by example. She was a warm, caring person, always putting the other person before herself. She used to prepare baskets of food for people, even though we ourselves had to make do with very little. Our one small room did not prevent us from having guests, especially for the *sedarim* on *Pesach*. My mother's good heart and sympathetic nature were lessons in themselves.

Binyamin, my older brother by four years, was a little hard for me to understand. My father must have been like him when he was a *bachur*. Although we used to play together when we were small, he lost all interest in me when he became *bar-mitzvah*. He was interested in learning and nothing else.

He had *chavrusos* that learned with him until all hours of the night, and he was a *masmid* in every sense of the word.

Binyamin had a beautiful voice. The *niggunim* he used to sing on *Shabbos* were absolutely heartbreaking. I loved to listen to him when he sang the haunting *chassidic* melodies that he knew so well. I was proud that my brother was such a good *bachur*. It made me feel as if I was important, too.

When my younger sister Sarah was born, things changed in the family. My mother became very sick, and she never fully recovered her health. We ended up moving to an apartment in a small village and commuting to Lodz to conduct business. Sarah was a year and a half younger than me, but we were still very close. I loved being the "big sister," and I felt it was my duty to take care of Sarah.

I had a wonderful family—an exceptional mother and father that I loved, an older brother that I idolized, and a younger sister that shared all my childhood secrets with me. It still hurts now to remember all that I have lost.

# CHAPTER 2

---■---

# Bnos Agudas Yisrael

W HEN I WAS NINE YEARS OLD, WE LEFT MY GRANDPAR-
ents' home and moved to a new apartment; my
parents had decided that the family needed a
little more space. The new apartment was on the first floor at
1 Kamienna Street, in the center of the city. I was delighted
with the move, because there were many girls in our new
apartment building. I was used to having only "babies" to play
with, and now I would have playmates much closer to my age.

I really liked the new neighborhood. The girls were very
friendly, even though they were a little older than I was.
Playing with them gave me a sense of being really grown-up,
and I was proud that they had accepted me into their circles.

It was one of the older girls, Sarka Cohen, who first
introduced me to Bnos Agudas Yisrael. We were playing ball

together when she suddenly stopped the game. Puzzled, I asked her why she didn't want to play anymore.

"I've got to go," she said.

"Where to?" I asked. "It's almost dark."

"I'm going to Bnos," she said. "It starts in a few minutes. Why don't you come along with me? I'm sure you'll enjoy it as much as I do."

I ran home and told my mother I was going with Sarka Cohen to Bnos, whatever that was. My mother liked Sarka, and she gave me permission to go with her. I ran back outside, and the two of us set off.

On the way, Sarka told me about Bnos. "It's an organization for girls," she explained. "There are lots of members, so we're divided into groups according to age. You can come into my group, if you'd like. I belong to Chuma Feldman's group. Don't worry, you'll like her. Everyone does."

Sarka was right. I liked Chuma from the very start. She was slim, short, red-haired and had a great sense of humor. As soon as enough girls were there, she gathered them into a circle and began to dance. I had never danced before, and I was too shy to join them, but Chuma drew me in and taught me the dance steps. My feet seemed to want to go in opposite directions. I wanted to leave the circle, but she wouldn't let me. She just grinned and said cheerfully, "Just try it again, Chanka. You'll get it this time."

Girls kept on coming and joining the circle. After a while, Chuma stopped the dancing and announced that the learning session was about to begin.

It was a group discussion, with everyone getting a chance to say something. All the girls were older than I was, and the discussion was a little over my head, but I was impressed with the way Chuma conducted the session. Each girl expressed her opinion, and Chuma listened to each one with the same lively interest. It was clear that she genuinely cared for every person in the room.

After the session, the girls got up and talked to each other. Sarka became involved with other girls, and I was left alone. However, I didn't find myself alone for very long. A girl came over and introduced herself to me. Her name was Chajusia Guterman, and she attended the same school I did. She was helpful and caring, and she went out of her way to make me feel good.

Chajusia had noticed my bewilderment earlier, and now she explained the topic they had discussed. As the days went by, she clarified anything I didn't understand, and I slowly became familiar with the subjects and began to feel more comfortable in my new environment.

When I first joined Chuma's group, it was the youngest in Bnos. As time went on and more and more girls joined, they were able to divide the group and form a new one for girls who were a few years younger. Since I was one of the youngest, I was transferred to a newly established group under the leadership of Guta Hendlish.

Guta's learning group started out with twelve girls, all of them my own age. The learning sessions were geared for my own age group, and I had no trouble understanding the material.

Bnos was a wonderful experience. The general program of Bnos Agudas Yisrael was mostly educational, and the sessions were usually conducted in the evenings. The leaders of the groups were generally girls who had completed seminary in Cracow under Sara Schenirer. The members of the groups were divided according to how much schooling they had and their level of comprehension.

31

We discussed both religious as well as secular subjects. We concentrated on *parshas hashavua, Neviim, Tehillim,* the meaning of various *tefillos* and the *hashkafos* of *gedolim* and *rabbanim.* All our *limudei kodesh* discussions were in Yiddish; when we had secular sessions, we spoke in Polish. Assignments were often given, and we would evaluate each other's work during our group discussions.

Bnos had its own newspaper, written in Yiddish and Polish. Material for the newspaper was provided by each individual group. Each member of the group could write articles, express opinions or relate the good news about a *simchah* in her family. The paper's special feature was the section of "Open Letters," in which girls could write to other members of Bnos.

Each group had a "Question Box" for notes and letters. The notes and letters could be anonymous, and the box was emptied every Tuesday. The girls would discuss the comments or questions raised without making anyone feel uncomfortable. If a girl felt a friend had done or said something wrong, she wrote a note and deposited it into the box. Only the person who had done it or said it knew the note was directed at her, and nobody was unnecessarily embarrassed. Without even realizing it, we learned what types of things made others unhappy, and we adjusted our own behavior accordingly. It was a very subtle *chinuch* that worked wonders.

The "Question Box" was just one of the many activities of our organization. Our program consisted of activities every evening of the week. Each evening had its own special schedule, whether it was learning some *Navi,* working on our articles for the newspaper, discussing current events, reading from the "Question Box" or learning a *perek* from the week's *parshah.* My favorite, though, were the sessions on *Shabbos.*

On Friday night, as soon as Mammeshe had lit the *Shabbos* candles, I ran to Bnos to *daven* together with the other girls. As soon as we finished *Maariv*, I hurried home so that I wouldn't be late for the *seudah*. I often met Tatteshe and Binyamin on my way home, since they davened in the Gerrer *shtiebel* right next door to Bnos. I felt very grown-up and special when I walked home together with them. I don't think I'll ever forget those wonderful moments—walking by my father's side as he entered the apartment, greeting my mother and my sister. During the *seudah*, my father and brother sang *zemiros*, and I proudly helped serve the meal. I loved the *Shabbos seudos*, but I couldn't wait to run back to Bnos for the rest of the Friday night program.

All Bnos members gathered in the large hall, impatiently waiting for the lecturer to come. In the meantime, girls of different ages mingled together, and I had a chance to get to know some older girls. There was a small membership charge for Bnos, and only members who had paid their dues were permitted entry to the lecture hall. My father always made sure that I had the money to pay my dues, so when the girl at the door let me pass, I felt proud to be a full-fledged member of Bnos.

The *shiur* was often given by a guest speaker, but sometimes the heads of Bnos spoke to us. The lecture was usually about the *parshah* of the week. After the lecture, people began to mill around, start a dance circle or meet friends they hadn't had a chance to see during the week.

We all had to leave by eleven o'clock in the evening. I raced home, waiting impatiently for the morning to return to Bnos again.

On *Shabbos* morning, at exactly nine o'clock, our group gathered to *daven*. Afterwards, our group leader translated and explained the meaning of the *Shabbos tefillos*. In the springtime, when it was warm enough, we used to take a walk to Poniatowski Park for our morning discussion. Then we hurried home to be on time for the *Shabbos* morning meal.

Between two and three in the afternoon we gathered again. This time we studied *parshas hashavua*. When the days were longer, we had time afterwards to talk and dance a little. *Shabbos* was a day full of happy activity, but the activities were always geared towards learning and *hashkafos*.

Bnos was an unbelievable experience. There were lots of girls whose parents were in the same position as mine—they simply could not afford to pay the high tuitions demanded by Bais Yaakov. I had to attend public school, and Bnos gave me my religious education.

It was Sara Schenirer who organized Bnos Agudas Yisrael, just as it was Sara Schenirer who recognized that when the Jewish education does not match the secular education, *neshamos* are in danger. She created Bais Yaakov to fill the void caused by the mandatory attendance of public schools in Poland. Would it be right for Jewish girls to learn secular subjects and not *limudei kodesh*?

Education in the home existed, to be sure, but the emphasis was always on the boys, not the girls. The influence of their Polish teachers caused many girls to become contemptuous of their "narrow-minded" brothers and fathers. Many became interested in the growing trend towards secularism, and there was a gradual drifting away from *Yiddishkeit* in general.

Then Sara Schenirer stepped in with her seminary in Cracow. She travelled all over Poland, securing permission from the *rabbanim* in each town before opening up a Bais Yaakov there. *Gedolim* gave her their encouragement and approval for her holy mission.

Suddenly, there was something to stem the tide of secularism and other pervasive influences. A Jewish education was possible! And for those who could not afford tuition, she created Bnos Agudas Yisrael as a non-profit organization so that everyone would have a chance to learn and grow in *hashkafos* and *Yiddishkeit*.

Frau Sara Schenirer must be given credit for the hundreds of thousands of lives she touched and enhanced, both with Bais Yaakov and with Bnos Agudas Yisrael. I know that I never would have survived the ghetto without the encouragement of the counselors and leaders of Bnos.

# CHAPTER 3

∎

# Summer Strike

**M**Y MOTHER HAD A VERY HARD TIME AFTER SARAH WAS born. She stayed in the hospital for twenty-two months, and she weighed barely more than I did when she was released. The medications and injections she had been subjected to on a daily basis had done nearly as much harm as good.

We spent two years in a small village, where Mammeshe had the peace and quiet she so desperately needed. Afterwards, we moved back to Lodz, but my mother's health was still very delicate. She was able to keep up with all of our antics, but her lungs couldn't handle anything strenuous. She didn't have any problems in the winter, but in the summer, she needed to get away from the smoke and pollution of industrial Lodz.

My father rented a cottage in the country. We lived in the cottage during the summer, when the heat was especially oppressive. My father used to commute back and forth to Lodz to oversee the weaving business that my mother, in an effort to supplement the family income, had set up when I was younger.

One *Erev Shabbos*, just two weeks before I started sixth grade, Sarah and I raced out of the cottage in our usual fashion when we spotted the telltale clouds of dust that told us that Tatteshe was coming. We greeted him in our *Shabbos* finery, each of us talking at the top of her voice as we tried to tell him the news of the entire week in less than ten seconds. My father smiled and chatted with us as he alighted from the wagon and strolled into the cottage.

He greeted my mother with his usual smile, but there was something wrong with his eyes. Something was terribly amiss, but he was trying to keep it from us. My father refused to let whatever was bothering him disturb the sanctity of *Shabbos*. He sang *zemiros* with his usual fervor, and he told us the story of the *parshah* with his typical enthusiasm. It was only on *Motzei Shabbos* that we overheard him speaking to my mother about returning to Lodz with him.

"Tatteshe, why does Mammeshe have to go back to the city in such hot weather?" I asked as I walked onto the veranda where they were sitting.

My father and mother exchanged glances. "Alta declared a strike," my father explained. "All the workers have stopped working, and the orders have to go out on time."

I was shocked. Alta was a close relative of my mother's who had been acting as manager for the weaving business in my mother's absence. She was practically a member of our immediate family, and I couldn't believe that she would

37

actually do this to us. She knew how hard it was for my mother to be in the city at this time of year!

"Why can't I go and take care of it?" I said impulsively. "That way, Mammeshe can stay here."

My mother blinked. "You're much too young, Chanka," she pointed out. "Besides, you don't have any experience, and you wouldn't know what to do."

"I can learn what to do!" I said stubbornly. "You taught Alta from scratch; you can also teach me!"

My mother said patiently, "Chanka, you're starting sixth grade in two weeks. You can't go to school and work at the same time, can you?"

"Yes, I can!" I insisted. "I don't have to drop out of school or anything. I want to help!"

My father looked as if he wanted to argue. Then he looked at my mother, at the circles under her eyes and the lines of exhaustion that were drawn on her face.

"Let's give it a try," he finally said.

That night, I was much too excited to sleep. At dawn I was fully dressed, impatiently waiting for Tatteshe. When I heard him moving around the bungalow, I quickly stuffed a few things into a bag and joined him in the kitchen. Half an hour later, we were on our way to the station where we would catch a train to Lodz.

The first few days on the job were very hard. It was hot and sticky, and I was so over-anxious to do a good job that I made lots of mistakes. By the end of the week, though, I was more relaxed, and I began to master all the little tricks of the trade. The second week was much easier. I was much more sure of myself, and my father persuaded some women, experts in their own right, to give me a hand. The business began running on a normal schedule, and I was almost "half an expert," as Tatteshe put it, by the time school started.

Although I had spoken very confidently when Mammeshe argued that I had school to worry about, I really had no idea how I was going to coordinate my daily studies with my work in the shop. I felt certain, though, that the whole thing would work out.

In the end, it all worked out beautifully. My sixth grade class only had sessions in the mornings, which gave me the afternoons to do work at home. I did my homework during the breaks between classes, so I only had schoolwork at home when I had to study for a test.

It wasn't a bother for me to work in the house. In fact, I think it gave me more confidence and self-assurance to know that I was doing my part. I worked the entire school year, and I graduated in the highest fifth of the class. Tatteshe promised me that next year he would send me to Ohel Sarah, a Bais Yaakov high school. I was so proud and excited! I had done so well, and now I was going to a Bais Yaakov!

From the perspective of hindsight, I find it ironic to think how excited I was that summer about going to high school. I had no idea that the fall months would bring a very drastic change to all our lives.

# CHAPTER 4

###### ■

# Bird Food

A UGUST, 1939! I WAS GOING TO START SCHOOL IN OHEL
Sarah in just a few weeks. There had been ominous
rumors of war and danger, but it seemed to me that
nobody really took them seriously. Life went on as normal.

We hadn't moved back to Lodz yet from our summer
bungalow. *Shabbos* morning, Tatteshe was running a fever—
completely unheard of! Somehow, children don't believe
their parents can ever get sick, and it was certainly a rarity for
my father to come down with some kind of illness. Mammeshe
was worried enough that she insisted on going back to Lodz
with him to make sure he was cared for properly.

My parents decided it would be better if we three children
would come with them into the city instead of staying out in
the country on our own. We all went back to Lodz, looking at

it as an adventure of sorts—a few days in the city, then back to the country for *Shabbos*!

The doctor came to our apartment and examined my father. He ordered him to stay in bed until Wednesday. My mother felt that my father should not be left alone, so we stayed in Lodz. Wednesday morning, my father was up and around, but he had to stay in the city until Friday to take care of business.

"We'll all go back to the bungalow together," my mother decided. "Another two days won't make a difference."

We went to sleep that Thursday night with excitement, planning to leave early in the morning. We woke up to the blare of a broadcast announcement coming from the court-yard where several men were huddled anxiously over a radio. Tatteshe went downstairs to investigate.

When my father returned, his face was white. Quietly, he told us what the broadcast had reported. Hitler had attacked Poland, and he was completely unstoppable. He was moving from town to town without any resistance whatsoever. All transportation was impounded for the use of the Polish army.

We were stuck in Lodz. I was upset that all our furniture and linens in the bungalow would have to be abandoned. I had no conception of war. My father and mother, who had lived through World War I, knew enough to be afraid, but we children were just annoyed that we were stuck in the city.

*Shabbos* passed quietly. Early Sunday morning, my mother dressed and left the house. She returned several hours later with a horse-drawn wagon loaded with sacks of potatoes in tow. A farmer got off the wagon and began to haul sacks of potatoes into the apartment under my mother's direction. I watched with surprise. Why was my mother stocking up on so many potatoes?

The same scenario repeated itself the next day, only this time she came back with a boy pushing a wheelbarrow filled with bags of a strange yellow grain. My mother stuffed the bags into every available spot, including under the beds, in the clothes closet and every other nook and cranny she could think of.

Puzzled, I asked her why she had bought the funny yellow grain.

She looked at me and sighed. "This is the only food I could get, Chanka. Everything else has been taken."

"But what is it, Mammeshe?" I asked.

"It's birdseed," she said quietly. "In times of hunger, one eats anything. May Hashem protect you from knowing hunger the way that I did in the last war."

I was really confused. It seemed very strange to be stocking up on bird food. I gave up trying to understand and just assumed that my mother knew what she was doing.

I found out quickly enough how foresighted my mother had been. It was only days before a shortage of food was felt in the city. The store shelves were empty; no provisions were available. Bakers were still baking bread, but the lines were already forming in the middle of the night. Any Jew spotted in line was dragged out by the Poles and beaten for his pains. So we ate potatoes and birdseed three times a day, and we thanked Hashem that Mammeshe had had the wisdom and courage to provide us with food.

Too young to comprehend the meaning of war, I decided I was going to go to the bungalow and see what could be salvaged. I was too stubborn to let anyone persuade me not to go. I tied a kerchief on my head, which made me look like a typical Polish girl, and left at daybreak.

There were no trains running, and I had to walk. A man

with a wagon gave me a ride, then changed his mind and ordered me off after only a few miles. Another wagon took me about halfway there, but from that point on, I had no ride at all.

The walking didn't bother me, but I was afraid of the young Polish boys who clustered around in groups, laughing and talking while they held flags with swastikas and wore swastika arm-bands. I had heard that swastikas were the German insignia, and it made me very nervous. I figured that the best thing to do was appear absolutely self-confident, so I looked straight ahead and walked with a sure, fast step, as if I didn't have a care in the world.

Finally, I reached our summer bungalow. I had been worrying about how I would transport everything back to Lodz, but I soon discovered that transportation would hardly be necessary. I arrived at the bungalow in time to see the Polish watchman carry out our last bed and place it in his storage shack. The bungalow was completely stripped of all our belongings. I would have to return home empty-handed.

The trip back to Lodz was miserable. I could hardly believe that what I had seen was actually true. Could people who had known us for years really do such a thing? It was my first taste of blatant anti-Semitism, and I felt very disillusioned.

I arrived in Lodz at dusk, absolutely exhausted. Passing Glowna Street, I saw a long line in front of a department store. I was desperate to have something—anything!—to show for my long day of useless effort, so I got on line. By the time I got into the store itself, all that was left on the shelves was some spaghetti. I purchased the one bag being offered per customer and walked out. Suddenly, it hit me that I didn't even know if the spaghetti was kosher. I walked over to the first person in line and asked her if she wanted it. Ten eager hands grabbed for the spaghetti, and I was glad to be rid of it.

Frustrated and tired beyond belief, I wearily made my way home. I poured out the whole story to Mammeshe, who only sat quietly and listened as I told her what happened.

When I finished my story, my mother shook her head and said in her soft voice, "Don't be sorry for things we lost, Chanka. Possessions can easily be replaced, and they're really not that important. The important thing is that you're back."

# CHAPTER 5

■

# Rude Awakenings

THE NAZIS MARCHED INTO LODZ ON SEPTEMBER 8, 1939. In their green uniforms, they reminded me of the plague of locusts in Egypt—swarms and swarms of them, seemingly without end. It was as if a cloud of disaster was enveloping us. It was a gray, sunless morning, and it seemed like the sun would never come out again.

The city went numb. The only sounds were the roaring of cannon fire, the high-pitched whistle of falling shells, the ominous tramp of marching troops and the rumbling of artillery over the cobblestone streets. All life in Lodz seemed to be smothered underneath the German beasts.

Thousands of refugees streamed into Lodz in the first days of the war, looking for shelter. They told us horror stories of what they had been through, of friends and relatives killed and people left on the side of the road to die. Many were wounded, some were suffering from shock, and all of them were starved and exhausted.

Despite the refugees' warning that running was useless, many people tried to escape Lodz. They literally bolted out of the city, with no set plan or destination; many of them were never seen again. Those that returned told of people machine-gunned by low-flying planes. There was simply nowhere to run.

In the early days of the war, I was still able to create my own dream world. Sometimes, I would read and take my mind off the horrible reality taking place all around me. It used to bother people to see me reading while waiting in line for hours at a time to get a piece of bread. I heard disgusted comments and got some very nasty looks. I was only trying to shut out what was happening to us. Why should that bother them? The truth was, though, that nothing could really shut out what was happening in Lodz.

One day, I felt as if the walls were closing in on me. I had to get out of the house and breathe some fresh air. I went cautiously out into the street, only to be caught up in the excitement of a crowd watching a procession of marching German soldiers.

I was too innocent to be frightened by the Germans, so I ran after the marchers so I could watch, too. When I got to Piotrokowska Street, I managed to stand on an elevated step and get a good view of our conquerors. I don't know why I had the impulse to see them, but I know that what happened next shattered something in me forever.

As the soldiers marched, they began to sing. I knew enough German to understand what they were saying, and I couldn't believe my ears.

"*Whenn Judenblut von messer spritzt, dann geht's nochmal so gut!* When Jewish blood spurts from the knife, then all goes doubly well!"

Mr. Schultz, one of our neighbors, was singing along with the Germans at the top of his lungs. He was wearing a German militia uniform with a shiny black swastika band. This was the man that was a friend of the family, the man who enjoyed my mother's cooking and used to join us for lunch on Fridays. And here he was, singing that horrible song with gusto! For the first time in my life, I knew the meaning of utter despair.

I pushed myself through the dense crowd and started home. The main avenues were filled with marchers and spectators, so I retreated to the quieter side streets. I couldn't get the picture of Mr. Schultz, our Polish "friend," out of my mind.

I had walked only five minutes when I heard gunshots. I whirled around in time to see two German soldiers pulling a man out of his house. They threw him to the ground and beat him savagely until he lost consciousness. A little further down the street, a cluster of Nazi stormtroopers strolled towards me while they amused themselves by shooting randomly into windows. I was surrounded by violence, and I was terrified.

My knees shook. I somehow kept walking, moving faster and faster until I was actually running. I kept ducking behind gates and crouching under steps, trying to hide. I found myself trembling uncontrollably. I stopped, taking deep breaths to calm myself, and told myself that it would be best not to run and appear afraid. Straightening, I resumed walking calmly and confidently, looking for all the world as if I had nothing to worry about. Utterly drained, I finally reached home.

The following days were ones of indescribable terror for the Jews. People were shot openly in the streets. Men were rounded up and driven to filthy stables, which they were forced to clean with their bare hands. Homes were plundered, shops were looted, Jews were maimed and broken. Panic spread through Lodz, and Jews no longer ventured from their homes.

The fear and excitement were very bad for my mother, who was very frail to begin with. She began having severe chest pains. My father went to the nearest drugstore to call a doctor. He was fully aware that he was endangering his life by going out into the street, but he also knew that my mother needed medical attention desperately.

I was afraid something would happen to my father. I should have gone with him! But I couldn't leave Mammeshe alone, either. I stood by the window, watching for him. I kept wishing I had gone with him; I would have been able to walk ahead and make sure there were no Nazis standing just around the corner. I would have been safe; they were looking for men they could put to work, not teenage girls. Why hadn't I gone?

I was still peering through the shattered window, straining to catch a glimpse of my father returning to the house, when I heard shots in the courtyard. I ran to the front door and opened it, but I saw nothing strange. I ran back to the window in time to see Mr. Schultz running towards our apartment, waving a rifle. In his haste and fury, he tripped on a thin piece of wood that protruded from a pile of firewood lying near the entrance of our staircase. Mr. Schultz went sprawling, and blood gushed from his hands and face. I stared, stupefied, as people came and took him away for treatment.

What had happened? I was replaying the scene in my mind, trying to figure it out, when I saw Tatteshe running home. He came into the apartment, speechless and trembling violently. He collapsed into a chair, completely incapable of saying a word.

After several minutes had passed, he calmed down to the point where he could tell us what had happened. While waiting to make his call at the drugstore, he had seen stormtroopers rounding up people. *Baruch Hashem,* the Nazis had found enough to amuse them on the streets and hadn't come into the drugstore to search for Jews. Thanking Hashem for sparing him from arrest, my father had made his call quickly and hurried back towards the house.

Once in the street, he sensed he was being followed. He started walking faster, and the person shadowing him did the same. Realizing that the person would soon overtake him, my father began to run. He was only a few feet away from our gateway when he heard someone shout his name. Shots rang out, barely missing him as he darted through the gateway. He dashed up the staircase, taking the steps three and four at a time, until he reached the attic.

My father knew, beyond a doubt, the identity of his attacker. He could hear the coarse voice of Mr. Schultz calling for him as the Pole followed him up the stairs. The attic, which had lines strung across from wall to wall for drying laundry, was completely empty. The only available hiding places were the storage areas assigned to each tenant, and these were crammed full with knickknacks and all the extras their owners didn't want cluttering up their apartment. My father ducked behind the open door of the attic and waited for the end.

Mr. Schultz came charging upstairs into the attic, yelling

with fury. My father could hear him slamming open the doors to the storage spaces, pulling things out and throwing them on the floor as he cursed and shouted. Forgetting the low ceiling in his anger, Mr. Schultz banged his head. Outraged and nearly demented, the Pole ran down the stairs into the yard, passing right by my father, and heading directly for our apartment. It was then that he tripped over that innocent piece of firewood and managed to knock himself out.

Why hadn't he looked behind the open door of the attic? Why had he tripped and fallen instead of forcing his way into our home and venting his frustration on us? Hashem was watching over us very carefully; it was a small bit of hope in a vast world of despair.

Tatteshe finished his story in a grim voice. He told Binyamin, Sarah and me to leave the apartment immediately.

"Take your overcoats and run!" he ordered us. "Mr. Schultz will be back, looking for revenge for his humiliation. Go to Zaidy's house, on the other side of town. Mammeshe and I will follow you soon."

My father was not about to leave the building without warning the other tenants of the possible danger. He knew that Mr. Schultz was perfectly capable of venting his anger on the other tenants of the building if we managed to slip through his fingers.

We children were shocked beyond comprehension. Besides the horror of the situation, we were stupefied by the actions of our supposed friend. Mr. Schultz had spent hours in our home! He had been like a member of our family. How could a person change so fast and so drastically from one thing to the opposite?

As time went on, we saw that it was typical for gentile "friends" to become bitter enemies and cooperate with the

Nazis in carrying out the final solution to the "Jewish Question." The Poles were very good at rounding up Jews for work and pointing out to the Nazis which Jews were well-to-do. They also informed the Gestapo of various places where Jews were hiding. Sometimes, they hid Jews in exchange for possessions and, after they had extorted all the Jews had, betrayed them to the SS. In many instances, Jewish parents paid their Polish neighbors large sums of money to protect their children and keep them safe; after these parents were killed, the gentiles gave the children to the Gestapo to be killed in turn.

The Nazis were very well aware of the deeply rooted hatred of the Poles toward the Jews. It was an essential element in the systematic and methodical extermination of the Jews. Why bother setting up extensive searches when the native Poles were eager and willing to point out all the Jews to them?

No, Mr. Schultz was not unique in his conduct toward the Jews. He was just one of many Polish gentiles who changed overnight, unleashing a suppressed, lifelong anti-Semitism.

# BOOK TWO

———■———

## The
## Storm
## Breaks

# CHAPTER 6

---

## Visits to the Hospital

THE GERMANS WENT ABOUT THEIR EXTERMINATION WITH frightening brutality. Jews were exposed to murder and assaults every hour of the day and night. Our home was no exception.

My mother suffered a heart attack when two SS soldiers burst into our apartment. Roaming around the house, they grabbed all our silver *kiddush* cups, my mother's candlesticks and my father's silver *Chanukah menorah*. Then one of them pulled my mother's wedding ring right off her finger, while the other held Tatteshe back, beating him with his rifle butt. When my mother saw the German point his rifle at my father, she fainted. After the SS men departed, leaving the house in a shambles, my father called a doctor, who had my mother admitted to the hospital.

I was the only one who would be able to visit Mammeshe in the hospital. The Germans were hunting Jews every day. They trapped them in the streets and sent them off to slave labor camps. Sometimes, they simply used them for their sadistic amusement, beating them mercilessly and plucking or setting fire to their beards and *peyos*. Neither my father nor my brother could go out into the street; the first Nazi that saw them would attack, and their *chassidishe* appearance made it even more dangerous. Sarah was too small and fragile to take care of things outside the house, so it fell to me to become the family's sole provider and link with the outside world.

On the night my mother went into the hospital, I worried constantly. Although I knew she couldn't stay home, I was afraid that something bad might happen to her in the hospital. My father told me she was the only Jewish woman there, and I knew Jewish life had no value. I had terrible nightmares about my mother that night. I found myself wanting to run to the hospital and convince myself that my mother was alive and that the Germans had not touched her.

The next morning, Sarah cooked a light soup for my mother. Since the only hospital available was a Christian one, we knew she would not eat most of the foods there. As soon as the soup was ready, I wrapped the pot in a towel, packed it in a basket and started out. I found myself shaking as I stepped onto the street. It was hazardous for a Jew, even a girl, to show her face in the city.

The streets were almost deserted. Here or there I could see a woman or child walking with hurried steps, anxious to get to her destination as soon as possible. Sometimes I saw a peasant woman, who had just come from her village, carrying a loaf of bread wrapped in a white cloth under her arm or in a basket. She was bringing the bread from the Aryan side of the city to sell it to the Jews. The peasant women knew what a precious commodity bread was right now—we ourselves were living on potatoes and birdseed—and they knew they could charge astronomical prices for a single loaf of bread. The smell of fresh bread made my mouth water, but I wrenched my mind away from it. I had to reach the hospital as soon as possible. Maybe my mother was hungry and anxiously awaiting my arrival.

I quickened my steps. I still had a long distance to go. Now the streets seemed completely deserted. The big apartment houses gave way to small one-family homes; no Jews had ever lived in this area. Some dogs were barking; my footfalls disturbed them. I could see some people staring at me from behind closed shades. I walked with a firm step, trying to look confident, but deep inside I was terrified. The emptiness and silence of the streets frightened me.

I was also frightened by thoughts of what might happen to my mother in the hospital. Poison could be put in her food, or she could be given a lethal injection. It would then be reported that she had died of natural causes. Who would worry about how a Jew had died? I found myself imagining the worst, and I started to run.

Out of breath, I stopped. When I had calmed down a little, I realized that I was standing right in front of the hospital. I took a deep breath and touched the towel which covered the little pot of soup. It felt warm; the soup would still be good. I told myself to be calm and natural for my mother, and I entered the hospital.

My mother was very weak but not afraid. She told me that the nurses seemed compassionate and that the other patients were too occupied with their own illnesses to show her any hostility. She thanked me for the soup and told me to tell

SISTERS IN THE STORM

Sarah how good it tasted. I felt relieved to see her so calm and hear how well she was being treated.

Her doctor, who was a German, told me she had suffered a slight heart attack and that her heart was enlarged. Even though the situation in Lodz was dangerous and uncertain, he felt that my mother should stay in the hospital for at least a week. He assured me that he would make sure she was well-treated. I felt a little assured, but not much. After all, how much could I trust a German after the last few weeks?

The week my mother stayed in the hospital was the longest in my life. Every day, new decrees were published, singling out Jews as undesirable citizens. I didn't trust that hospital; my mother was the only undesirable person there. My fears for her well-being increased, because the terror in the city grew worse and worse with every passing day. The Jews lost all protection of the law. But at least the Jews were together! Yes, things were miserable, but it's much easier to bear suffering when you have others with you. My mother was all alone in that hospital, in a neighborhood that was completely German. I breathed a long sigh of relief when Mammeshe finally came home.

At that time, a new order was announced. All Jews were to wear a yellow armband, identifying them as a member of the lower, undesirable species of human beings. Disobedience to the decree was punishable by death. Its intention was clear; if Jews were easily identified, they would be easier targets for the Germans.

More decrees followed. One declared that Jews were not to show their faces in non-Jewish sections of the city. Yet another decree forbade Jews to walk on Piotrokowska Street, the most luxurious and busiest Jewish street in Lodz. Jews who were prepared to pay for the privilege, however, could buy permits to walk on this street. It was just another example of how the Germans were determined to get every scrap of value out of the Jews before killing them.

These were the conditions under which we lived for about three or four months. We were beneath the protection of the law and apart from other human society. We were denied any possibility of existing as normal people.

Following hard on the heels of the yellow armbands came the yellow star. We were ordered to wear a yellow star on the front and back of each garment when we went outside. More obvious than the armbands, the yellow stars were also a means of humiliation and embarrassment for us.

Then, after restricting us from walking on most Jewish streets, the Germans listed the hours we were allowed to walk at all on the permitted streets—between eight o'clock in the morning and five o'clock in the afternoon. Anyone caught on the streets after curfew was sent away or summarily shot.

Thousands of Jews tried to escape to other towns, seeking some kind of relief, but they found out it was futile to try to escape the Nazis. Poland was completely crushed beneath the German armies. It seemed that we were completely without hope.

# CHAPTER 7

■

# The Walls Close In

I N MID-DECEMBER, RUMORS STARTED TO SPREAD THAT THE Germans wanted to make Lodz *Judenrein*, free of Jews. Just the sound of the word sent chills down my spine. Free of Jews? Would we have to move? Where to?

I didn't understand that *Judenrein* could have a much more menacing meaning than simply being forced to move.

Jews, alarmed when the rumors did not subside, tried to escape. There wasn't much that could be done; unless a family had a great deal of money, the Poles refused to do anything to help, and without a gentile's help it was completely hopeless. Polish anti-Semitism assured us that we couldn't expect help out of kindness or sympathy. All the *goyim* were interested in was making money.

Lodz had been a bustling, happy Jewish community.

There were over sixty Jewish schools—both *cheder* and Bais Yaakov—and over twenty thousand students. There were old-age homes and orphanages, *batei midrashim* on every corner and many organizations of *gemilas chassadim*. Jewish newspapers, in Yiddish and in Polish, were published daily. The Jewish *kehillah* was vibrant and productive in Lodz—that is, until Hitler came on the scene.

It had already begun in 1934, when local fascists were elected on a platform of freeing Lodz of the "Jewish scourge." Anti-Semitism, which always lurks right beneath the surface, was coming out in the open. Then, with the start of World War II, things took a drastic turn for the worse.

When the Nazis invaded the country in September 1939, the three million Jews of Poland fell into Hitler's bloodthirsty hands. The Germans were much too efficient to carry out the solution to the "Jewish Question" by merely killing every Jew in sight. First they would rob them of all their possessions, deprive them of their humanity and squeeze every ounce of strength out of them. When the Jews were no longer capable of performing their forced labor, the Nazis would annihilate them completely.

To achieve their goals with maximum speed and efficiency, the Nazis established the ghettos. The first of these was Ghetto Lodz. We were their very first experiment, and it was an honor we would have been much happier without.

On February 8, 1940, the Ghetto of Lodz was established. We were all herded into Baluty, the poorest, filthiest and most neglected section of the city. There were already several thousand Jews living there, but now the entire Jewish *kehillah,* fully a third of the population of Lodz, would be forced to live within Baluty—180,000 Jews crammed into an area of one and a half square miles.

During the period of transition, all the gentiles living in the designated ghetto area were ordered to move out, while the Jews from other parts of Lodz moved in. We had to leave our homes without delay. Clothing, furniture, linens, silverware, china—everything had to be left behind. Merchandise had to be abandoned in stores that were already being looted by gentiles. Even before the ghetto was fully established, a complete lack of human dignity was imposed upon us in every conceivable fashion.

I'll never stop having nightmares about our move to the ghetto. I can still see flashes, as vivid as if they had happened yesterday. The mothers with crying children at their sides, pushing tables turned upside-down as a "sled" filled with the family's belongings. People with large bundles tied to their backs, bent nearly double under the weight. Men clutching parcels of *sefarim* and *tallis* and *tefillin*, afraid to let their most precious possessions out of their sight. And the eyes! I still shudder when I envision those eyes that were filled with calm despair and the knowledge that this was truly the beginning of the end.

It took days for us to move into the ghetto. It wasn't just the horror of it all that took its toll. The weather added to our anguish and conspired with our cruel enemy. The frost bit our faces and froze our breath, and the violent wind tugged at shabby clothes and head coverings. The temperature readings were twenty-five degrees below zero.

I felt helpless, horrified, degraded and humiliated, thinking of what awaited us in the future. What kind of life would we have? Could it even be called living?

I watched the procession and thought of how we might bring our belongings to the ghetto. This was actually less of a problem than how to get my mother there; she had barely recuperated from her heart attack. I stood on the street and watched other families milling about, feeling utterly confused and lost. The situation was hopeless. Even if my mother would have been able to walk the distance—and she couldn't—the cold was too much for her.

Where could I turn for help? Everyone was in the same predicament. Everyone was marching in the same miserable condition. Young and old, the sick and the lame, all were stolidly plodding on as they blew on their palms, shaking their feet violently to keep their feet from freezing. Every single person trudging towards the ghetto needed help. Where could I get help for us?

A sudden idea flashed through my mind. I could try the Linas Hacholim! It was an agency, partially supported by the *kehillah*, for people with medical needs. I was familiar with the place, since my mother's condition was such that we had often needed their help. I decided to go there and ask them to provide transportation for my mother.

When I got there, it was obvious that I was not the only person who had thought of going to the Linas Hacholim for help. The office was jam-packed with people looking for assistance. I had a hard time squeezing myself past the front door. Once inside, I decided I would not budge until I got what I came for. I waited impatiently in line. Finally, I was able to present my case to one official, but he hardly seemed to listen. I repeated my request, stressing how frail my mother was, but he told me coolly that there were many Jews in the city with problems and he simply could not take care of mine.

For just a second, I believed him. Maybe I was being too egotistical and selfish. There were so many sick and weak, so many people in the same situation that needed help just as much as we did. Who was I to think that my favor should be granted? Then I shook my head. I was not asking anything for myself. I was asking for help for my sick mother! No, I had every right to ask for assistance. I wiped away my tears of shame, straightened my back and was ready to resume my quest.

The officials were running back and forth, looking harassed and flustered. The commotion was so great that I could hardly hear myself think, much less speak. For a while, I didn't approach anyone. I just watched to see how the various officials acted towards the people who came to Linas Hacholim to ask for help.

I noticed one young man in particular. He spent more time with people than the others did. Others, evidently noting the same thing, had formed into a long line to speak to him. I got on that line, eagerly awaiting my turn.

The line moved very, very slowly. People were chafing at the delay, but the expressions on the faces of the people who walked away from the young man's window made the long wait seem worthwhile. If only I would look that hopeful when I was done speaking with the official! If only I would get a chance to speak to him at all! The clock was spitefully ticking away the minutes, and I knew that the sympathetic young man would not sit in his place forever.

Just as I reached the window, the young man leaned forward and announced that he was finished for the day. I couldn't believe my ears. It was finally my turn, and he had to stop now? The people in line behind me started to shout and scream, but the young man apologized and left. One by one, the other officials left, too, until there was nobody of any authority in the office at all.

The Linas Hacholim, which had been the scene of frenetic activity only ten minutes before, was now completely deserted. Other Jews, who had come desperately seeking help, left in despondency and resignation. Not me, though. I didn't move. I couldn't move! I told myself that it would be better to sleep in the streets than go home without accomplishing what I had set out to do.

I began opening doors in the deserted building at random. The doors were all unlocked, but that wasn't much help; the rooms were empty. Then I found one door in a corner that looked like an exit and opened it.

There I saw a woman in her thirties, sitting at a table, in a room that looked like it had originally been a closet. She looked at me, surprised, but she invited me in cordially enough. I walked into the room, and she pulled out a chair from behind her desk and told me to sit down.

The last thing I had expected was kindness, and it opened the floodgates. All the misery I had tried to bottle up broke loose, and tears filled my eyes. The woman sat patiently and let me cry. When was the last time someone outside the family had treated me with common dignity?

When I was finished crying, I told the woman my problem. She listened to me without interruption, her eyes open and sympathetic. She thought for a few minutes, then she asked me to wait until her future husband came in. He would be able to tell her the best way to help me.

After about ten minutes, an older man walked in. She told him my story. He looked at me, studying my tear-streaked face. Then he turned to his future wife and told her to go ahead and make the phone call. As she started dialing, the man nodded at me, smiling, and left the room. The woman spoke into the phone in rapid Yiddish, then turned to me and said that a *dorozhka*, a horse-drawn carriage, would be waiting for me outside in the street. I wanted to say something to thank her, but the words stuck in my throat and I could not force them out. The woman looked at me with open warmth in her eyes, and somehow I knew she understood. The man who approved the *dorozhka* was Chaim Rumkowski, the *Judenelteste* of the Lodz ghetto.

I didn't believe it was actually happening until I placed my foot on the small step and mounted the carriage. When I rode into our courtyard, my parents were even more shocked than I had been. There was still a whole hour until sundown, but we had to rush because of the curfew. I quickly grabbed the two down quilts. I put one on the seat as a cushion for my mother, and I wrapped the other one around her to keep her warm. I put some of her essential things in the carriage—her medicines, her bedding and some linen. I climbed onto the carriage step and gave the driver my uncle's address. Uncle Fishel lived in the section of the city where the ghetto had been created, and he would surely take us in.

I can still feel the anger and shame that welled up inside me when we joined the procession to the Baluty section of Lodz. The only street the Germans allowed us to use in our relocation was packed with people, rich and poor, who were being forced to leave the homes in which they had lived all their lives. Very few of them had a place to which to go. They were simply running away from death, and death would reach them, sooner or later.

To add insult to injury (the Germans were very good at doing that), any Jew had to move aside to make space whenever a vehicle had to go by. We weren't allowed to use the sidewalks in the first place, so it made things doubly difficult. I felt terribly guilty to be forcing my fellow Jews to move aside for me. Standing on the step of the slowly-moving carriage, I felt worse than if I had been part of the crowd on

foot. Wasn't there anything we could do? Was blind obedi-
ence to orders all we had left? Why were we so utterly helpless
to do anything? I was miserable, angry and frustrated by the
time we finally reached Uncle Fishel's apartment in the heart
of the Baluty section.

When we arrived, it was already evening. We found many
of our relatives there. Nearly all of our family in Lodz had
gravitated towards Uncle Fishel's apartment. We were twenty-
seven people, crammed into an apartment consisting of an
average size bedroom, an average kitchen and a children's
room that was actually converted from a walk-in closet. We
were warmly welcomed by the whole crowd, but it made me
very nervous to see how everyone looked so worried about
my mother.

Arrangements for the night were such that most of us
slept on the floor. My mother was given the table to sleep on.
It was actually the best place under the circumstances. Sarah
and I slept on the floor under the table, right underneath her.
There was almost no air to breathe; not only was the apartment packed but the children's room and bedroom had
sloping ceilings under which only a child could stand up
straight. It was stuffy, hot and miserable. But then I remembered that there were hundreds of Jews tonight that did not
have any shelter at all, and the circumstances were suddenly
more bearable.

# CHAPTER 8

■

# A Place to Live

I WOKE UP IN THE MIDDLE OF THE NIGHT TO HEAR MY mother gasping for breath. She needed air, but the room was so stuffy I could barely breathe myself. Frantic, I pushed the window open to let in some air. Fresh air came into the room, along with a fierce swirling of snow and cold. I couldn't even force the window shut. I was shivering violently in the cold, and I was terrified that my mother would catch pneumonia. Panicked, I grabbed the first things I saw and piled them on top of my mother. She started coughing, and all I could do was watch her suffer, praying silently that she would make it through the night.

The next morning, I awakened Binyamin and told him what had happened. He agreed with me that we had to find separate lodging for our family. Another night like that and

Mammeshe could, Heaven forbid, suffer another heart attack. Tatteshe gave us money, and Binyamin wrapped his
face in a shawl so that his beard and *peyos* didn't show. It was
such a cold day that we figured it wouldn't look suspicious.

Binyamin and I went from house to house asking if there
was any apartment available for rent. There was nothing to be
found. All homes in the center of the ghetto were taken, and
there was no way we would be able to find an apartment.

Binyamin suggested that if we ventured closer to the
Aryan side, we might find something; few Jews wanted to risk
being exposed to the enemy. We weren't all that interested in
being exposed to the Poles, either, but we had to do what was
best for our mother.

The sun had risen by that point, and the snow had
stopped falling, but the frost was terrible. Shivering, we
walked as quickly as we could toward the outskirts of the
ghetto boundaries. As we drew further and further away
from the main concentration of Jewish homes, I became
more and more uneasy. Binyamin, who noticed how tense I
was, asked me what was bothering me.

"Oh, Binyamin," I sighed. "Can't you see what's happening to us? The Nazis hunt us down like animals. We can't even
act like human beings anymore. What are we supposed to
do?"

"Chanka," Binyamin said in his calm voice. "Tatteshe
taught you Jewish history. You've told me that you learned
history in Bnos, too. So you ought to know that this ghetto is
not the first one. The Nazis aren't being original, Chanka.
There were ghettos before. The Jews have always suffered
from persecution. We are but one link in the long chain of
our history of suffering. The only difference is that now it is
we ourselves who happen to be the link in that chain. When

you read those stories, Chanka, when you learned about the Spanish Inquisition and Chmelnicki's Cossacks, you could tolerate the pain they suffered. Now it's we who are suffering. Now that we're involved, you understand the pain that existed all along. I think that now is the time to learn to be strong, to know how to act in the face of our suffering and to understand the meaning of our suffering. The *Ribono Shel Olam* knows what He's doing, Chanka. Don't ever forget that. The Germans want you to, but don't ever, ever forget it."

I listened to Binyamin in silence. He was right. The *goyim* have always wanted to crush us, and this time was no different. The Nazis' aim was to destroy our faith as well as our bodies, and we had to do everything we could to be sure they did not succeed. I envied my brother; he was so confident in his *emunah*. I wished my *emunah* was as strong as his.

Involved in our discussion, we did not realize we had reached a sparsely populated area. The houses were small here, with little gardens and tall trees. We stopped at a fenced-in garden, with a huge tree with spreading limbs and a wooden bench. I thought to myself that a bench under a tree in a garden full of flowers was exactly what my mother needed.

Binyamin seemed to read my thoughts. "This is exactly what Mammeshe needs," he said as he pulled the wire bell at the low wooden gate.

A gentile woman came out and asked what we wanted. She seemed very condescending; after all, she knew that she would soon be living comfortably in a spacious apartment outside the ghetto boundaries. Binyamin, ignoring her superior tone, asked politely if she would be willing to let us rent part of her home.

She looked us over appraisingly before offering to allow

us to rent part of the house for three hundred *zlotys*. I couldn't believe that she had the audacity to demand such a price. Why should she ask us for so much money when she knew she would get a luxurious Jewish apartment for no money at all?

As I opened my mouth to say something, Binyamin stopped me. "Would you let us move in today if we gave you a partial payment right now?" he asked her.

She looked at him narrowly before she answered. "Yes, I will. And if you pay me the full amount now, I'll also leave you two iron beds."

I started to speak, but again Binyamin ignored me. He gave her the money, and she led us into the house. We came into a room that measured ten by fourteen feet. There were two windows looking down into the garden. The room was completely empty except for the two iron beds, both standing against the long wall of the room. The fact that the room was otherwise unfurnished made me realize she had already moved out before we came and was only waiting for an opportunity to squeeze more money out of the Jews. She was only doing us the great favor of giving us the two beds because they were probably too heavy for her to carry.

I was furious with Binyamin for giving in to her and letting her take advantage of us. There was no doubt that Binyamin knew how angry I was, but he ignored the look on my face entirely. He pocketed the key the woman gave him and wished her well. Together, we walked out of the house and started home.

As we walked back to Uncle Fishel's apartment, Binyamin answered all the silent accusations I had been making. "Chanka," he said firmly, "it doesn't matter if that woman took advantage of us or not. What matters is that we got exactly what we wanted."

71

"That's true," I admitted grudgingly.

"There's something more important to remember, though. We are approaching a new phase in our lives, and we have to learn how to act, especially with the *goyim*. And think of something else, Chanka. How does that woman feel? Yes, she will be resettled in a home that will probably be much nicer than the one she's giving up. But sometimes the grandest apartment cannot take the place of a poor home when the home is taken by force. She, too, is being forced to leave her home. It is important that we look to see the significance of even the smallest things that happen to others, or the Nazis *have* won, for they have caused us to become low, greedy animals without the slightest concern for another."

I stopped and looked at him. I didn't know how to put my feelings into words. Binyamin was more prepared than I was to cope with our new life. His calm and wisdom, his firm answers to all my agonizing questions, were ample proof of this. His determined resolutions were exactly what I needed. If the purpose of the ghetto was to crush us spiritually, then I knew that Binyamin would be a bulwark of spiritual strength for me to lean against in the harrowing months that lay ahead.

# CHAPTER 9

---■---

# Defiance of Death

HARROWING WAS CERTAINLY THE WORD FOR IT! ON May 1, 1940, the Lodz Ghetto was sealed. The suffering we went through was almost beyond belief. The Nazis believed that by subjecting their victims to inhuman conditions they would cause them to commit suicide en masse or kill each other. Those who insisted on surviving would die from starvation and disease instead. We Jews were, indeed, quite stubborn about survival, but the starvation and diseases worked out all too well.

Our nights and days were filled with misery, deprivation, disease and starvation. Hundreds of people died daily; I felt like we had all forgotten how to smile. What was there to smile about, anyway?

Hunger was the great plague of the ghetto. It was a

chronic disease which destroyed the victim's body and mutilated the mind. The lack of food threatened to totally absorb our consciousness during all our waking hours. The pain of hunger oppressed and deprived us of peace and nearly drove us to insanity, to the extent that the central focus of existence became food. Trapped behind wire fences, living in squalor and filth, subjected to savage brutality, we lived under conditions in which any other type of people would surely succumb to despair.

But the Nazis made one big mistake—they forgot that they were dealing with Jews. Instead of being driven to suicide when we were faced with total annihilation, we looked for avenues of resistance. Even under the shadow of extermination we clung to life, totally contradicting our enemy's line of reasoning. Isolated from the outside world, we turned inward instead.

As soon as the ghetto was stabilized, elementary schools and high schools were established. *Chumash, Navi* and Jewish history were among the many subjects taught. Almost every child in the ghetto came to school. Even those that had attempted to become assimilated before the war lost all interest in being like the *goyim*. What was the point, when it was so obvious that the *goyim* considered them Jews? Many of the children of these so-called "enlightened" Jews joined the newly-organized ghetto schools to learn something of their precious and ancient Jewish heritage that their parents had tried to throw away.

In a way, it was the most stubborn form of resistance we could have possibly chosen—insisting on living when the Nazis wanted us to die. They wanted to destroy our will power and faith; we laughed in their faces and established *minyanim* and *chaburos* for learning. The sounds of Torah rang through the streets of the ghetto, sweet sounds of life in a place that was otherwise deathly silent.

Bnos had been disbanded, but it reorganized in the ghetto, with learning sessions conducted in private homes. There was one particular *tzaddekess*, Fayga Zelicka, who was a former student of Sarah Schenirer and never let a day pass without a session of learning. She lived in Marishin, a section of Lodz that had been annexed to the ghetto, and girls used to walk in snow and rain, an hour or even more, to attend her sessions.

My brother Binyamin was the perfect example of the profound resistance of the *frum* Jews of the ghetto. He was twenty years old when the wire fences went up. Refusing to compromise his standards and values even the slightest degree, he was less concerned with his physical survival than with his spiritual survival.

Uncompromising by nature, and always ready to fight for his convictions, he joined a *chaburah* of boys his own age. They studied *Gemara* from early morning until late at night, learning with the same *hasmadah* and intensity they had applied before the war. They couldn't be bothered to go home during the day to eat; each member of the group brought what little food he received as his ration and put it in a common bowl. They all ate while singing and telling *chassidishe* tales.

I envied their communal meals. I knew that they could turn a meager supper into a feast with their enthusiastic spirit, songs and stories. It gave me comfort to see Binyamin and his friends full of confidence and hope in the face of all that was happening to us.

I remember one time when my mother prepared *seudah shelishis* for the entire group. The whole family had been involved in saving the pieces of bread and the potatoes that would make up the *seudah*. Binyamin had been saving bread for weeks; he would cut a piece off his daily slice of bread, wrap it in a handkerchief and place it in a drawer. When the pieces added up to an entire slice of bread, he would eat the pieces and add the whole slice of bread to his growing store. My mother contributed two potatoes, a kohlrabi and a bit of flour, which she cooked into a soup. She also saved him some beet leaves. She fried the leaves in a little oil—the ghetto equivalent of fried fish. I was very excited, and I waited impatiently for *Shabbos* to come.

Binyamin hung blankets from the ceiling in one corner of the room to form a separate, miniature room for the *seudah*. He fit a table and some stools into the small room he had created. From the attic above us, he took down some boards, balanced them on the stools, and improvised two benches. Before the other young men came, my sister and I helped him set the table. We still had a white tablecloth to make the table look more *Shabbosdik*. We put the food on the table—the bread, the potatoes and the "herring" my mother had made out of beet leaves. Then Sarah and I withdrew from the little "room" to watch from behind the makeshift partition of blankets.

At the appointed time, the members of Binyamin's *chaburah* arrived—ten young men, each dressed in *chassidishe* garb. They all brought some food with them, and the food was placed in a tray in the middle of the table. My mouth was watering. I figured that they would sit down and eagerly eat everything in sight. They sat down at the table, but instead of eating, they started to study! They plunged into a lively argument about the *mesechta* they were learning. They were so involved in their discussion that they didn't even seem to realize that the food existed. The meal wasn't important to them—their learning was.

I peeked at them from behind the blankets, and I realized that they were resisting the Nazis in a way the Germans would never be able to counter. How could Germany ever defeat *bachurim* who didn't even pay attention to the suffering and hunger?

After they had finished studying, they washed their hands and started to eat. Even when they ate, their minds weren't on food. They sang *Shabbos zemiros* to the haunting *chassidishe* melodies. Their enthusiasm kindled a spiritual light in our house. For a moment, as I listened to their voices sweeping upwards and praising Hashem for all His good works, I forgot my own hunger. The *zemiros*, the *seudah*, the young *chassidim* themselves were like something out of a beautiful dream.

The *bachurim* lifted themselves out of the ghetto darkness. They spontaneously jumped up from the benches to dance around the table. From behind the blankets, I could see their faces, their glowing eyes and their flushed, hollow cheeks. They were in a transcendent, spiritual realm, much closer to heaven than to earth. That *seudah shelishis* will forever be one of the few bright spots in the memory of my life in the ghetto.

After Binyamin and his friends left the apartment to go to *Maariv*, I realized that their gathering had actually been an act of rebellion. They had completely defied the Nazis. The suffering, the fear, the pain and hunger that we all felt did not drive them to despair; on the contrary, they stubbornly insisted on keeping their faith. Instead of following the orders of the Germans, they followed the orders of the Torah. They were able to find strength, meaning and light in the darkness that enveloped us. I felt that Binyamin had, once again, taught me a very important lesson. Our defiance of the Nazis was in refusing to give up the *Yiddishkeit* they were trying to tear away.

# CHAPTER 10

■

## The Relief List

UNFORTUNATELY, THERE WERE JEWS WHO WERE EAGER
to help the Nazis, thinking that this would save them
from the horrible fate that threatened to engulf us all.
They turned out to be only too wrong in the end, but before
they died themselves, these Jews caused unbelievable harm to
*Klal Yisrael.*

Our ghetto, too, had its share of Jews who acted that way.
Mordechai Chaim Rumkowski was given the role of *Alteste,*
chief administrator of the Jews, by the Germans. He himself
was subordinate to the German mayor of Lodz, whose
intention was to squeeze every drop of usefulness out of us
before having us deported. Perhaps we are wronging
Rumkowski, and he was deceived by the Germans himself;
but those of us who were there can't help but think that he

used our suffering for his own personal advantage.

He controlled the property of the ghetto. The fate of all of its inhabitants was directly in his hands. When demonstrations broke out, he could call on German troops to shoot down the demonstrators. He was also authorized by the Germans to impose a tax on the ghetto inhabitants. He was truly the "Jewish dictator" of Ghetto Lodz.

One of Rumkowski's strongest beliefs was that work would save the people of the ghetto. One of his more frequent slogans was, "Work is our passport to life." Two weeks after the ghetto was sealed off, Rumkowski submitted a letter to the German mayor informing him that he had completed the registration of 14,850 skilled workers. He attached a list of over seventy articles which the ghetto would produce for the benefit of the German economy. Soon afterward, shops and factories, called "resorts," were established in the ghetto to produce these goods.

Thanks to Rumkowski's organizational efficiency and his drive to please the Germans continuously, Ghetto Lodz came to be considered an "exemplary ghetto." In no other ghetto was there such colossal productivity. It is quite possible that this was the reason the Lodz ghetto was the last to be liquidated.

Even though Rumkowski did us a great deal of good by making us into such an exemplary ghetto, we should have become suspicious when he established the zasilek—a relief list for the unemployed, about eighty-five percent of the ghetto population. He said that anyone registered on the list would receive financial aid. Why didn't we react with skepticism towards his generosity? Why didn't we realize that the man who insisted that the ghetto be a hive of production would not want to waste money on the unemployed for nothing? No one thought about it, though; everyone simply needed the money too much.

I was only sixteen years old. I didn't have the experience older people had, but I felt that I should warn everybody not to take the money Rumkowski offered. There had to be something wrong! There had to be some kind of trick involved! But who would listen to me? I had no inside information. I was just a teenager with a hunch, and there was no way I could convince anyone that I was right.

I tried to argue with Tatteshe and Mammeshe, who were already calculating what we could buy with the money we would get every month. I did not agree with their idea of blindly accepting Rumkowski's welfare.

"Tatteshe, why do you think he wants to support the unemployed?"

"He's a Jew, Chanka." My father looked at me, surprised. "A Jew always helps another Jew in times of need."

"But he's always telling us that we have to prove to the Germans that we're all productive. It just doesn't fit! Why would he waste money on people who aren't working? It just doesn't go along with everything else he ever says and does!"

"Chanka," my father said patiently, "you're probably right. I don't understand it either. But let me ask you a question . . ." It was then that I could see the pain in his eyes. "How do you expect our family to live? What will keep us from starving if we don't get on Rumkowski's list for financial aid?"

I looked at my father. He had been through so much! My mother's health was poor. He couldn't get any work as a *sofer* in the ghetto. He was trying so hard to keep the family together, but how could we survive if we had no income at all?

"I'll find work, Tatteshe." Was that me talking?

81

"You, Chanka?" My father stared. "What kind of work will you find to do here in the ghetto?"

"I'll find something, Tatteshe. I will! Just please, please, don't put your name on Rumkowski's list!"

My father was silent for a few moments. There were tears shining in his eyes as he slowly nodded his head. He would not put his name on the *zasilek*; he would trust me to find some source of income.

I don't know what prompted me to act the way I did. Why did I act so strongly because of an intuition? I had no idea how I would carry out my plan; I didn't even know how to start. My compulsion to reject the *zasilek* was a reaction to an inner voice which told me that the *zasilek* was the prelude to a great tragedy. I wasn't sure of myself at all; my apparent self-confidence was plagued with fear and doubts. What if I did not succeed in finding a job, and then it was too late to register for welfare? I was determined, though, to make sure that nobody in our family would be part of the *zasilek*. I had faith in Hashem that I would somehow find a way to bring in the money we so desperately needed.

Early the next morning, I left the house without telling anyone where I was heading. I was determined to find a job somehow. I had no idea what I was qualified for, much less what was available, but I was somehow sure that I would find something to do so that my parents' names would not go on the *zasilek*. Actually, I didn't tell anyone where I was heading because I didn't know myself. I needed to think in the open air.

A bright and shining sun met me on the road to Marishin. Why did I choose the road leading to Marishin? I do not know. Maybe it was because that was where Fayga lived, where I had often attended Bnos learning sessions, and I felt a little more comfortable there; or maybe it was just Hashem putting me on the right path. All I knew at the time was that I felt like I needed fresh air and a clear sky. Marishin was the only place in the ghetto where there were real trees and live flowers, where the air was filled with the fragrance of growing things.

My lungs expanded as they took in the fresh early spring air. I gave a sigh of pleasure as I came across a lovely garden. There were low bushes with tiny green tomatoes, radish beds, new cabbage and carrot plants, a bed of proud-looking scallions, and young cucumber vines springing from the dark, wet soil. This was the first time since the ghetto had been established that I had seen so much of nature in one place. To whom did this lovely garden belong?

As I stood there, entranced by the lovely sight of the garden, I suddenly felt someone touch my arm. Turning, I was surprised and delighted to see my best friend Lubcia Leiserson standing there with her older sister Surale.

"Lubcia! I haven't seen you in ages. What's been happening? How are you—"

"Let's take her with us, Lubcia," Surale interrupted impatiently.

"Where to?" I asked, puzzled.

"We'll tell you as we go. Come on!"

"Where are you two rushing to at this early hour of the morning?" I asked in astonishment. We were literally running along.

"We're going to work, and we're late. We're almost there. You can walk home afterwards." Surale knew that once Lubcia and I started to talk, we would never finish. She dragged me along with them so we wouldn't waste time.

We stopped at a shack full of work clothes and garden

tools. Hurriedly, they changed into some of the clothes. They seemed to have completely forgotten me. I just stood there and stared. They had jobs! I was so desperate to find something to do, and they both had work! They grabbed their tools and were about to run out of the shack to their jobs, when I suddenly burst into sobs. I just couldn't hold back my tears any more.

Surale thought she might have offended me and started to apologize, but when I told her the real reason for my crying, she asked me to wait while she spoke to her supervisor. Ten minutes later, I was standing in the office of a tall young man, who handed me a working suit and a pair of garden tools.

I had a job! A real job! I could hardly believe it. I had to pinch myself to make sure that I wasn't dreaming. *Baruch Hashem*, there would be no need for Tatteshe and Mammeshe to put their names on the *zasilek*! The work was back-breaking, especially since I was completely inexperienced, but I felt so happy just to be working that it didn't seem to matter. Nobody's back ever hurt with as much pleasure as mine did at the end of my first day on the job. Even my blisters were worth it!

I was glad that we had a source of income. I felt relieved that my anxieties over the *zasilek* had been unnecessary. Now that we no longer had to depend on it, I could laugh at my fears. Surely I had been wrong to think the *zasilek* was dangerous.

I only wish that I had been wrong! If only my suspicions had been incorrect! If only Rumkowski had been sincere, and the *zasilek* would have been exactly what he claimed it was— a list of people who received financial aid from the leaders of the ghetto.

Unfortunately, my hunch turned out to be correct. When the Nazis demanded the first large transport of ghetto inmates for deportation, Rumkowski had a list all ready for them, with a convenient excuse for slating them for deportation. After all, these were the "unproductive" people of the ghetto. The efficiency of the ghetto would not be lessened by their disappearance at all. All the Jews whose names were on the *zasilek*, as well as their immediate families, were thrown into trucks and never seen in Lodz again.

# CHAPTER 11

———————■———————

## Warring over Wood

T HE COLD, WHICH HAD BEEN MISERABLE COMPANY during our terrible trek to the ghetto, was even worse throughout the entire winter. There was no fuel to heat the one room in which we lived; there were no rations of wood or charcoal. The Jews in the ghetto took to cannibalizing anything and everything to get wood so as not to freeze. Cabinets, closets, beds, chairs—anything made out of wood simply wasn't safe from the axe. Some of the more desperate took to pulling wood out of fences, sheds and even houses for fuel. Even stealing went on in the ghetto; the tenants of one house near us got up one morning only to find that the stairs had vanished during the night, along with the handrail and the banister.

The house we had rented from the Polish woman was also

wooden. We weren't the only tenants; there were six other families in the house, three per floor. The attic, which was right above our heads, had long, smooth, wooden floorboards. Sarah and I had spent many hours playing up there, trying to forget our hunger.

Once we found a loose panel up in the attic. It was a bitterly cold day, and here was a piece of wood that we could burn to warm ourselves with. We looked at each other. We knew that it was stealing, but surely it was a case of *pikuach nefesh*! We couldn't freeze, could we? Deep down inside, we knew that we were just rationalizing to ourselves; we knew it was wrong. But we took that panel down to our apartment and fed our stove. The warmth made us feel very good for a few minutes, but the guilty feelings lingered for days. I remembered what Binyamin had told me, how important it was to stay strong when the Nazis were trying to destroy us, and here we were, doing what we never would have dreamed of doing in happier days.

The winter dragged on, with no prospect of relief in sight. The walls of our room were covered with ice. How were we supposed to live like this?

Things took a sudden turn for the worse when Mammeshe developed a fever. Sarah and I made up our minds; this time, it really *was* a matter of *pikuach nefesh*. There was no way we were going to let my mother, sick as she was, shiver in a freezing room without any hot water to drink. Slowly, one at a time, we pried the floorboards up from the attic and brought it down to our apartment. Our consciences did not allow us to pull out any boards that were not directly over our heads. That way, at least, we weren't causing other people to suffer by removing the shelter from over *their* heads.

It did not take long before we discovered that we were not

the only ones dismantling the attic. Often, in the middle of the night, we could hear someone ripping up boards and carrying them down the attic ladder. Inevitably, any protection from the elements our roof had provided disappeared. The real problems began when the snow started to melt and water leaked into our apartment. Later on, in spring, we suffered terribly from the rain; the floor turned into one big puddle.

Things weren't any better for us the following winter. We had to start ripping out our own floor. Stealing wood had become a literal epidemic in the ghetto. Because the problem was becoming so widespread, Rumkowski put his foot down and announced that anyone convicted of stealing wood would be sentenced to several months in prison. Everyone knew it was only a very small step from imprisonment to deportation.

One frosty night, my father went over to a friend's house for his nightly learning *seder*. He came home after midnight, half-running through the blowing snow, and quickly got ready for bed. He had already fallen asleep when the banging started on the front door.

Sarah, who was a light sleeper, woke up and went to the door. Mr. Bilander, a neighbor from across the street, was standing there, looking tense and nervous. Without a word, he brushed past Sarah and knelt by my father's bed, shaking him awake.

Bilander begged my father not to tell anyone what he had seen. My father, half-asleep, didn't know what Bilander was talking about. He mumbled something and tried to turn away, but Bilander persisted. He offered to give some of the wood to Sarah, as long as my father wouldn't tell anyone what had happened. My father, who still wasn't really awake, motioned Bilander to go away.

Bilander turned to Sarah and told her to come with him. Sarah was confused. What wood was Mr. Bilander talking about? What did it have to do with Tatteshe? Still, it was fuel, so she followed Bilander down the stairs and into the yard, where he handed her several pieces of wood. Sarah didn't understand why he was being so generous, but she was delighted with the prospect of having a little more warmth in the house. She ran back up the stairs, piled the wood near the oven and went back to sleep.

The next day, when Sarah was coming home from work, she was approached by two Jewish policemen who demanded to see her identification. She nervously showed them her identification card. A quick glance was all they needed before they dragged her off to the police station. She was thrown into a room where two officials were toying with long, vicious whips. Their intentions were very clear—either she would confess to helping Mr. Bilander steal wood the night before, or she would find out what it felt like to get a beating.

Sarah was absolutely terrified. She had never seen the inside of a police station before, much less been accused of a crime she hadn't committed. She was so frightened that she couldn't even open her mouth to deny the accusation.

They thrust a paper at her and commanded her to sign it. Too bewildered to even think, Sarah did as she was told. It was only after her signature was safely on the statement that they told her what she had just "admitted"—that my father had conspired with Mr. Bilander to steal wood the previous night and she had been sent to collect my father's share of the wood. They escorted her out of the room and sent her home.

Only when she was standing on the street did Sarah fully realize what had happened. She had signed a statement that implicated Tatteshe, and there was nothing she could do to deny it. Worse, she *had* gone to Mr. Bilander to get some wood; that part of the story was true and would make it look like the rest of it was as well. Mr. Bilander had been arrested for ripping wood out of a fence, and he had implicated my father as his accomplice. And now Sarah had signed a statement that confirmed Bilander's accusation!

Sarah panicked. She ran home to find neighbors waiting for her in the apartment. They gently broke the news to her: Tatteshe had been arrested that morning. He was in jail, with Sarah's signed statement hanging over his head like a death sentence.

We sat down together and tried to figure out what had happened. We talked over the events of the night before, trying to piece the puzzle together. We realized that Bilander must have stolen some wood, and he must have thought that my father had seen him stealing it. He tried to bribe my father into keeping quiet by offering to give him a share of the stolen goods. Someone else must have spotted Bilander ripping the wood out of the fence and reported Bilander to the police. When Bilander was arrested, he must have thought that my father had gone to the police, and he implicated my father as his accomplice out of spite.

Now Tatteshe was in jail! What was going to happen? We knew there was going to be a trial, but what chance did Tatteshe have of getting a fair trial in the ghetto?

Sarah and I spent the next few weeks saying *Tehillim*. Poor Sarah couldn't sleep nights; all she could think of was that it was her fault that Tatteshe was in prison. We could only *daven* to Hashem that everything would turn out all right.

With the help of our neighbors, we put together our defense. The three men my father learned with were going to come to court to testify that my father had been with them the entire night and couldn't possibly have been busy stealing wood. One of the neighbors, who had been a law student before the war broke out, coached Sarah on what to say when she was giving testimony. He pointed out that there was a big difference between Bilander giving her "pieces of wood" and Bilander giving her "part of the wood"; the former indicated a gift, while the latter indicated participation in the crime. There would be somebody else on our side, too—the person who saw Bilander stealing the wood and reported him to the police.

The day of the trial came. When the attorney called the first witness to the stand, we couldn't believe our eyes—it was our own super! Bilander had ripped the wood out of the fence right outside our house, and our super had seen him doing it. He declared that there had been no sign of my father anywhere. Bilander's face turned white. He had no idea that the super had seen him; he thought it was my father who had accused him.

Then my mother was called to the stand. She was pale but composed as she told the judge how Bilander had come into the apartment in the middle of the night and asked my father not to say anything. Binyamin and I were also called up, and we confirmed what my mother had said.

When Sarah took the stand, she was calm and sure of herself, in complete contrast to how nervous she had been at the police station. She clarified very firmly that Bilander had given her some pieces of wood, not part of the booty as he claimed. She was completely convincing. The attorney could do nothing to shake her.

I watched Mr. Bilander's face as my father's *chavrusos* took the stand. Unexpectedly, I felt a sudden wave of pity for him.

I thought I would hate the man who had caused us so much trouble, but I couldn't help feeling sorry for him. After all, why had he stolen wood in the first place? It wasn't as if he was trying to start some kind of business with stolen goods; he was just trying to get a bit of wood to warm up his apartment or boil some hot water for tea. Is this what the Nazis were doing to us? Pitting Jew against Jew to the point where one man would be willing to condemn another to death?

The trial ended with Tatteshe a free man, while Mr. Bilander was sent off to the labor camps. I thought about Mr. Bilander for a long, long time. He had been deported—sent to his death—for the crime of stealing a few boards of wood. Was it such a terrible thing to do? Did he really deserve to be sent off to die? Then it hit me. Yes, of course it was a terrible crime! After all, if a Jew had wood to warm his home, he would take that much longer to freeze to death! In the eyes of the Nazis, Mr. Bilander had been guilty of the greatest crime of all—a Jew having the temerity to try to survive.

# CHAPTER 12

■

# Not the Children!

I T WAS DURING THAT SAME TERRIBLE WINTER WHEN THE Nazis first demanded a transport of Jews for "resettlement purposes." The people on the *zasilek* were among the first ones to be taken. We were told that these people, who were unemployed, were going to be resettled in another area where there were jobs available. The alternative to believing what they told us was just too awful to bear—so we believed them! Hashem help us, we believed them!

The first *Aktion*, or roundup, began on January 15, 1942. It lasted nearly two weeks, and anybody that was deported was never seen again. Ten thousand people were taken away to their deaths. Ten thousand people! How can one understand what that means? How can one feel the despair of a child who watches his father walk out of the house and doesn't know if he'll ever see him again? Even now, I can't help shivering whenever I remember the horror of those terrible, terrible winter days when families were torn apart forever. The streets weren't safe. Our homes weren't safe. Nothing, nobody was safe! Anybody could have been taken away, and ten thousand were—ten thousand people, murdered in the death chambers of Chelmno.

It didn't end there, either. The Nazis ignored the original promise they had made to the *Alteste* that there would be only one "resettlement." They demanded larger and larger numbers of Jews for deportation. The spring months became one long, unbearable nightmare, and there was no way we could wake up. It wasn't just the people who were on the *zasilek* anymore. All the members of that person's family were taken, and then anyone else living in the same apartment, and then anyone else living in the same building. The net spread wider and wider. Life became a deadly game of cat and mouse, moving from one place to another to elude the roving bands of Germans. We all knew that if we lost the game, there wouldn't be any second chances.

Inexplicably, there were no deportations during the hot summer months. We walked around the ghetto in a daze. There was hardly a single room in the entire ghetto where someone was not sitting *shivah*. We tried to get back to normal life (as normal as life can be in the ghetto, that is), but the reprieve lasted only a few short months. In August, the rumors began to circulate again. There would be another *Aktion*, and it would be quick and vicious. It was *chodesh Elul*, and I felt like the next few weeks would really show how we would be written down for the coming year—*mi yichyeh umi yamus*, who would live and who would die.

This time, there wasn't even any pretense of taking

people for a purpose. Small children were snatched from the streets, and elderly people were dragged from their beds to be thrown onto the trucks. There was no rhyme or reason. It was just sheer cruelty. Then came the worst of all.

It was a warm sunny morning—September 1, 1942. The entire ghetto was quiet, almost too quiet, as if we were all holding our breaths. Then, with perfect synchronization, trucks pulled up in front of every hospital in the ghetto.

In the previous deportations, patients had generally been left alone by the Nazis. This time, though, they were the primary target. Nurses and doctors were roughly pushed aside as the patients were mercilessly dragged out of their beds and off the operating tables to be thrown into the waiting trucks.

Some medical personnel tried to argue; they were shot for their pains. Others managed to hide several patients from the Germans who roamed the hospital wards, searching for Jews. In all, two thousand patients, including four hundred children, were taken in the *Aktion*.

Hysterical mothers struggled frantically to reach their children. One of my friends told me that she saw one mother shot when she was only inches away from her daughter. Another mother, trying to get to her five-year-old son, was graciously allowed to hold him in her arms—while she herself was thrown into a truck to join the others being carted off to their deaths.

But it wasn't enough. The Germans still weren't satisfied! They demanded that all the children in the ghetto be added to the transport. They gave Rumkowski the order—any child under ten must be taken. The Nazis wanted to make sure that there would be no future generations of Jews to trouble the world.

Rumkowski knew that the job was impossible. How could he persuade the parents of the ghetto to give up their children? He called us all together for an emergency meeting. I managed to find a crate to stand on, so I had a perfect view of his face when he told us that we would have to surrender anyone who was ill as well as all children under ten to the Nazis. It is traditional, he said, for one part of *Klal Yisrael* to give itself up so another part would survive—and he told us that we would be doing the same by giving up our children. The sick are doomed anyway! Let them die so that the healthy will live! We have to give so many Jews to the Germans—let us give them the children and the sick, so that we may save our lives!

The shouts of horror drowned out what he was saying. How could he possibly claim that giving sick people and children up to be killed was a part of *Klal Yisrael*? I felt like I was choking. Give up the children? Please, Hashem, not the children!

Then Rumkowski made an offer. Anyone appointed as a "soul snatcher"—any person who would be an official assistant to the Nazis in taking the children—would have their children exempted. In return for condemning other children to death, their own children would be saved from the deportation.

And so it was that the Nazis succeeded once again in pitting Jew against Jew. In the *shpero*, as the roundup came to be called, the Jews who had been appointed as "soul snatchers" became fanatical machines with hearts of stone. Driven frantic by the desperate desire to save their own children from death, they had no hesitation in searching homes and brutally dragging shrieking children away from their families.

The nightmare lasted for an entire week. The Nazis, losing patience, grabbed people off the streets at random—anyone who had gray hair, or was too short, or had too many wrinkles, or anything else that struck their fancy. All too often, they simply opened fire on the streets, killing hundreds whose only crime was that they happened to be nearby.

It still wasn't enough. The next step was a house curfew. Nobody was allowed on the streets, period. The ghetto was divided into seven sections; each section would have an entire day devoted to searching it out for any potential victims. The Gestapo and the Jewish police went from home to home, selecting Jews for death. Anyone who tried to evade the selection fell under a hail of German bullets.

Each block would be surrounded by trucks. Nobody even wanted to breathe; the only sound was the tramping of heavy boots. Children were dragged out of their homes, screaming with terror. Any mother who tried to fight was shot instantly. Any mother who insisted on going along with her child was thrown into the truck and added to the number of victims. There seemed to be absolutely no way out.

Throughout that entire second week of roundups, there was no food distribution at all. The only thing we had was water. Sarah and I tried to joke about it, but a week of nothing but water left us starved and listless. Once, the distribution center near our home had potatoes; hundreds of Jews ignored the curfew and came to get something for their starving families. The whole project ended rather abruptly when the Nazis appeared and opened fire on everyone standing in line. There was nothing we could do except force ourselves to choke down yet another glass of water and wait miserably for the *shpero* to end.

Our home, situated on the very edge of the ghetto, was in

the seventh and final section. Sarah and I were terrified. Even though we were both over ten, we knew that the Germans were taking older children and teenagers as well. *Baruch Hashem*, we were left unharmed, and the *shpero* was finally, finally over.

Or so we thought.

# CHAPTER 13

———■———

# Five Small Potatoes

I SPENT MOST OF THAT NIGHT STARING AT THE CEILING. I knew what the next day would bring—long lines at the food distribution centers. I was relieved that we would finally have something to eat, but I really hated standing in line. I was very unassertive; I couldn't bring myself to argue with someone who cut into the line in front of me. The curses that were hurled on my head the few times I managed to actually open my mouth were more than enough to discourage me. More often than not, I would end up with nothing to show for my pains, because all the people who had slipped into line in front of me had taken what was left.

I racked my brains, trying to think of a way to get food that wouldn't involve the distribution centers. It seemed such a pity that I was earning money but couldn't buy any food.

Of course! I sat up in bed. The fields of Marishin, where I worked, had several garden plots. With the recent upheavals in the ghetto, I was sure that the fields were unguarded. It would be simplicity itself to sneak into the fields and collect some potatoes and beets to put on the table.

I slipped out of bed and quietly woke Sarah. The two of us dressed in silence and left the house without disturbing anyone. The sun was just coming up, and there was nobody else on the streets. My feet were swollen, and we were both drained from the long week we had just gone through, but we ignored all our aches and pains. The two of us were excited over the prospect of bringing a few vegetables home, and it made the long walk seem almost pleasant.

It was only when we had nearly reached the fields that I realized that something was wrong. The green of the fields was gone. Usually, I could see flashes of green ahead of me, but everything seemed as brown and dreary as the rest of the ghetto. I stared at the denuded fields with dismay. Sarah, standing beside me, voiced what I was thinking.

"It was a wonderful idea, Chanka," she sighed, "but you weren't the only one to think of it. Other people have been here before us, and now the fields are empty."

I looked at her pinched, white face. My heart went out to her. "Let's take a look anyway," I suggested. "We might be able to find something that the others missed."

There were dozens of people in the fields, but we all very carefully avoided looking at each other. Sarah and I moved a few feet apart and started to dig. At first, the results were very discouraging. The fields had been dug up so deeply that there were actually pits in the ground, holes so deep that several people could fit inside. After a while, though, I found a small potato. Excited and encouraged, I continued digging,

100

and I found another one. I showed Sarah the fruits of my labor, and she proudly displayed the three potatoes that she had dug up herself. Pleased that we would not be returning empty-handed, Sarah and I started picking our way through the fields towards home.

Suddenly, a car drove into sight. A man, leaning out the back window, was waving at us urgently and shouting something. We couldn't understand what he was saying, but we both knew that something must be wrong. It must be a warning! What was going on?

As the car drove past, the man shouted desperately, and this time we could make out the words. "*Uciekajcie! Uciekajcie! Schowajci sie!* Run! Run! Run and hide!" We stared, stupefied, and then turned to run. But it was too late.

A loud rumbling shook the ground. A cluster of German trucks came to a stop, right on the edge of the fields. The *shpero* might be over, but the Nazis weren't ready to leave us alone.

Hashem, help us! Had we survived two weeks of horror only to be cut down in the fields of Marishin?

The fifteen trucks had come to a halt on a spot that was literally only a hundred feet away from me. SS men jumped down and began shooting. The dozens of Jews in the fields were completely exposed; there was no shelter in sight. People bolted through the grass, completely in the open, with Nazis carrying machine guns at their heels.

I was too numb to think. I must have decided that I was going to die anyway, so why run? I actually sat down on the grass, waiting to be shot, when Sarah's voice, which seemed to be coming from a great distance, jarred me back to my senses.

"Chanka! Run, run! He's right behind you!"

Sarah had been running deeper into the fields along with everyone else when she realized that I hadn't moved. Now she stopped, waiting for me to catch up with her. I tried to move, but my feet felt like two lumps of lead that insisted on staying right where they were. I desperately wanted to collapse, but I couldn't. Sarah was waiting for me, even though there were literally bullets flying over her head.

As I stumbled closer, Sarah realized that I could barely walk. She became terrified and began flailing her arms wildly as she jumped up and down in a panic. I'll never forget what she looked like. It was as if she was doing some kind of macabre dance, beating her legs with her fists and making whimpering sounds as she watched me collapse on the ground, too exhausted to move any further.

I waved violently, trying to get her to move. She just stood there, her whimpers growing louder and louder. She was only thirteen. If a seventeen-year-old can go to pieces, why couldn't she?

I had to get up. I couldn't let Sarah just stand there and get shot down!

The whole episode must have taken only seconds, but it felt like an eternity—Sarah standing there while I crawled towards her, the shouts and screams coming at us from all sides as Jews dropped like flies.

She was saying something, but I couldn't hear her; the noise of people dying was overwhelming. When I got close enough, I could hear what she was saying. She was mumbling the same words over and over again.

"What should I do? What should I do?" She seemed oblivious to the death that surrounded us.

"Left, Sarah!" I shouted hoarsely. "Run to the left!"

She wouldn't budge until she could see that I was coming,

too. She ran ahead a little bit, then waited until I finally caught up with her. Then we staggered on together, Sarah half-supporting me as we ran.

To this very day, it is beyond my comprehension how Sarah and I managed to survive. Hashem must have made those Nazis blind! Perhaps it was because we were only two young girls, and there were much better pickings for the Germans on the other side of the fields. At the time, though, all I knew was that every second might be our last in this world.

We stopped for a moment to catch our breaths.

"Where should we go?" Sarah asked.

I was panting so badly that it took a moment before I was able to talk. Trying to reassure myself as much as her, I reasoned that the Germans wouldn't be interested in us.

"There are only two of us," I said. "Since everyone is running ahead, it does not pay for the SS men to follow us." As I spoke, I realized that it actually made sense. I felt myself relaxing, and Sarah looked calmer as well.

Keeping low, we moved farther and farther away from the sound of gunfire. We were crawling through high grass now, and we were actually hidden from sight. Sarah seemed to think that I knew where we were going, but I was just moving as far away from the Nazis as I possibly could.

Suddenly, shots rang out in our direction. I thought I was too drained and exhausted to be afraid anymore, but I was wrong.

Terrified, we stumbled to our feet and tried to run. I couldn't keep up with Sarah. My feet were so swollen I could barely walk, much less run. I tried to motion for her to go ahead, but Sarah grabbed my arm and refused to let go. I don't know where she got the strength, but she pulled me along so fiercely that she was actually dragging me behind her.

We were stumbling straight ahead towards the place where the other Jews were trapped. Suddenly, on impulse, I veered towards the left, where a small path showed in the dirt. Sarah tried to tug me back in the other direction.

"Where are you going?" she hissed fiercely. "We have to join the others! It's the only way we'll be safe!"

I couldn't agree with her. Maybe logic was on her side. Isn't there safety in numbers? I'd learned a long time ago, though, that logic just doesn't work in the ghetto. The only way to survive was to act on instinct, and right now all my impulses were shrieking at me to stay as far away from the other Jews as possible.

"This way," I insisted as I pulled her to the left.

"There are houses up ahead!" she said in a hoarse whisper. "Those are the sheds where they keep the tools and work clothes. We can hide inside there, and be safe!"

"Sarah," I said through clenched teeth, "the Nazis will look in the sheds to see if anyone is hiding there. We have to stay out here, where nobody's looking. Besides, we can't cross the open field to get there. They'll see us and shoot!"

We had taken only a few more steps when we heard the sound of booted feet coming near us. We both froze. Sarah's body started to shake, and she was gasping for breath. She mutely pointed in the direction of the sheds. Her eyes were begging me to go there, but I refused. She didn't look like she could move, but I yanked on her arm, and she slowly started moving again.

There was nowhere to go. No place to hide. The thumping sound of the soldiers' feet seemed to come closer and closer. Sarah looked back in terror; I looked for a miracle.

Hashem, how could I have doubted You? There it was, right ahead of us—our miracle. It was a small clearing, perhaps three feet square, almost directly ahead of us. Unless you were looking directly at it, you couldn't tell it was there; it was almost completely hidden by the tall grass.

Tugging Sarah towards the clearing, I threw myself onto the ground, pulling her along with me. Sarah didn't seem to realize what I was doing. Protesting against the mud, she tried to rise.

I held her down fiercely. "Stay down!" I whispered into her ear. "We're going to lie here until they're gone. They won't be able to see us." I kept a firm grip on the collar of her coat so that she wouldn't be able to get up, even if she wanted to. *Baruch Hashem,* her coat was green; it was almost the exact same shade as the grass that camouflaged us on all sides. The road was only a few feet away. Would our hiding place be safe enough?

We could hear the SS men close by now. They were running, and at one point we actually caught a glimpse of a rifle held high in the air, right above us. One of them must have seen somebody; he shouted in German and fired his rifle. Sarah and I huddled together in terror. Then they were past us, and silence engulfed the field.

An hour passed, the minutes crawling slowly by. Sarah became impatient; she kept raising her head to see what was happening, and I kept jerking her back down. We had no idea if any SS troopers were still nearby.

"Chanka, what will happen to us now?" Sarah whispered.

Irritated, I said the first thing that came to my mind. "The Nazis must suspect that people are hiding here. They will set machine guns along the road and kill everyone they see."

Too late, I realized how terrible that would sound to poor

Sarah. She stared at me, eyes wide with horror, and began to whimper with fear. I gently placed my hand over her mouth to keep her quiet. If I was right, we definitely couldn't afford to make any noise.

Sarah's eyes were just beginning to lose that look of panic when we heard a sound in the grass. Keeping my head down, I peered through the grass and saw one of the Nazis ruffling the tall grass with his rifle, trying to find people who might be lying out in the fields. I broke out in a cold sweat. I huddled closer to Sarah, hugging her tight. Please, Hashem, let him walk away!

It took forever, but the German eventually moved out of our immediate area. Now the stillness of the field was broken by the sound of motorcycles sputtering their way towards the work sheds. A line of trucks rolled up behind the motorcycles. We watched as people were dragged from the work sheds and thrown into the trucks. Sarah was shuddering convulsively; she had wanted to find shelter in the work sheds, and look what was happening!

We watched Jews asking the Nazis to spare their lives. One young mother volunteered to walk into the trucks voluntarily, if only they would let her baby boy go in peace. Both of them were shot on the spot. The Germans didn't even look at the bodies as they stepped over them to throw more Jews into the trucks.

When the trucks were full, they were driven off. They weren't gone for long; they came back just ten minutes later, completely empty. They must have been driven to the deportation center, and it must have been close by for the trucks to return so quickly. The Nazis made very good pickings. Forty trucks full of Jews were deported from the area. Finally, the last truck rumbled off, and silence returned to the fields. It was utterly quiet, almost as if nothing had happened.

Were the Nazis finished? Was it over? Soon afterward, we heard loudspeakers blaring. *"Akcja skoczona!* The *Aktion* is ended!"* It was an announcement to inform one and all that it was finally safe to return to our homes.

When Sarah heard the announcement, her eyes lit up. She jumped to her feet, but I yanked her back down. I still didn't trust the Germans. I wasn't ready to reveal our hiding place. I extracted a promise from Sarah that she would not move until I told her to. And I wouldn't tell her until—until what? I didn't know.

How I wish I had been wrong!

Many of the Jews that had not been caught in the fields had fled for safety into the pits—dug up by people searching for food. Now, when they heard the announcement, they emerged from the darkness of the pits—into the greater darkness of death.

It was as if the Germans had sprouted from the earth! One moment, the only people visible were the Jews climbing out of the holes in the ground. The next moment, bloodcurdling shouts echoed through the fields as the SS stormtroopers pounced upon their victims. Those poor Jews had survived the harrowing weeks of the *Aktion* and had managed to escape the initial roundup in the fields. And now they had been trapped by a miserable trick. The trucks, which were hidden behind the work sheds, were quickly filled up. They drove away, leaving silence behind.

Sarah and I watched as the children hiding in the pits were brutally kicked and shoved into the trucks. We stared as adults were beaten over the head and bloodied into submission. We looked with dull eyes as the trucks drove away. It was all we were capable of doing any more.

The sun was high in the sky; it was already noon. A relative calm spread over the bloody field. We got on our knees and looked around. The regular field guards, who were supposed to prevent anyone from raiding the gardens, had taken up their positions around the borders of the field. The Nazis were really gone this time.

We picked up the bag with the five small potatoes that we had found early that morning and started back. When we reached the edge of the fields, one of the guards stopped us. We looked at each other, then we handed him our potatoes. Without saying a word, we quietly walked home.

# CHAPTER 14

■

## Slipping Sanity

I T WAS WISHFUL THINKING TO EXPECT THE *SHPERO* TO BE the last deportation. There was another *Aktion* every few months, and each one had its own particular target. One was a deportation of "singles"; another was random, when people were snatched off the streets without rhyme or reason. Then there was the *shtichtag*, when any person who missed a particular day of the week was taken away. The factor of uncertainty was yet another weapon designed to beat us into complete submission. There would be no respite from the deportations until the entire ghetto was liquidated.

My brother Binyamin didn't let this stop him. He continued his learning sessions, he insisted on keeping all his *chassidishe minhagim,* and he decided to continue on with life—by getting married.

I couldn't believe it when I first heard it. A *chasunah?* In the ghetto? To me, it seemed like the most ridiculous thing I had ever heard. Binyamin's outlook was different. His faith in Hashem was incredible. He was not going to let the Nazis stop him from living an ordinary life, and part of an ordinary life was finding a wife. He would marry Brocha and raise children to be strong in Torah and *maasim tovim.*

It was only a few days before the *chasunah* when I realized that getting married was probably one of the greatest acts of defiance that Binyamin was capable of. So the Germans wanted to exterminate us? He was defying them by continuing on with life, by getting married and having children in spite of their brutal desire to wipe us off the face of the earth. They want us to disappear, but we would add to our numbers! After that reasoning, I was able to watch with a little more peace of mind when Binyamin was standing under his makeshift *chupah.*

I still had mixed feelings, though. Binyamin was leaving us! He and his wife Brocha were moving to the other side of the ghetto. I wondered uneasily how I would cope without Binyamin to inspire and encourage me. What was going to happen?

All too soon, I had more important things to worry about. We had been in the ghetto for eighteen months when my mother fell ill again. She tried to hide it from us. She told us she was coughing because she had a bad cold, and she didn't tell anyone that she was running a fever. But when she started coughing up blood, she couldn't hide her condition any more.

Mammeshe was bedridden. I used to sit by her bed, holding her hand tightly. I was so afraid! Please, Hashem, don't take Mammeshe away. I need her so much!

I watched helplessly as she grew weaker and weaker. Tatteshe couldn't even get me to move away from her bedside. I was afraid to leave her, even for a second. It was as if I could sense how little time Mammeshe had left.

Then it happened. It was a gloomy *Shabbos* morning, chilly and gray. Mammeshe looked pale and wan as she lay in bed. I raised her up gently, trying to make her more comfortable. She leaned against me and gave me a faint smile. Her mouth moved, as if she was trying to say something. Then she turned her head to the side, let out a faint sigh and slowly closed her eyes.

Her head slumped on my arm.

She was only forty years old.

I went through the week of *shivah* in a daze. I must have been awake, but I could have been asleep for all the interest I took in everything that was happening around me. Nothing mattered. I just didn't care. The worst thing of all was that I couldn't cry. I watched Tatteshe as he sobbed at the funeral. I watched Binyamin standing with Brocha, tears streaming down his face, but my eyes remained dry.

I knew I was going to have to go to work, but I couldn't bear the thought of facing life again. I couldn't stand the idea that Mammeshe wouldn't be sitting quietly in her chair, that look of calm understanding in her eyes, giving me strength to face the horrors of life in the ghetto.

When the seven days of *shivah* were over, I was supposed to go back to work. I didn't. I didn't even get out of bed. I wrapped myself in my thin blanket and stayed in bed all day, staring at the ceiling.

I watched the shadows deepen on the ceiling. The day was already over. The tears I'd been choking on for the last eight days welled up and constricted my throat. I clenched my teeth. What was the point of crying? Mammeshe was gone. Binyamin was off and married. Who was there to comfort me?

"Tonight is *shtichtag*. Anyone who misses work might get taken for deportation. If you don't go to work, you might get on the list."

I looked up, startled, at the sound of Sarah's voice. It was the first time I'd heard her speak in eight days.

I didn't answer her. I didn't want to think about work, and I wasn't sure I would be able to say anything without bursting into tears. I stayed in bed for a few minutes longer, wishing I could just stay there forever, but I knew that Sarah was right. I couldn't take the risk. Anyone who was not at work on *shtichtag* could be put on the next list for deportation, along with the rest of their family. I would have to go.

Slowly, I climbed out of bed and began to dress in the gathering darkness. I noticed vaguely that my clothes were shabby and torn. It's been three years, I thought drearily, since I've had something new to wear. And now, there's no one to mend my dress for me.

A sudden ray of light flared through the window. Someone must have just lit a lantern across the courtyard. The thin ray of light fell fully upon Mammeshe's black coat with the silver fur collar. Then the light disappeared, leaving us in darkness again. I was left with the picture in my mind's eye of that coat hanging by the door. Without really thinking about it, I walked over to the coat and touched it gently. Very slowly, I took it down from the nail. Then I was burying my face in the soft fur of the collar, breathing deeply.

A feeling of warmth and security suddenly engulfed my whole being. I felt as if this coat was my link with my mother.

I took another deep breath, taking comfort from her scent.

The light switched on suddenly. Sarah, who was already dressed, gently took me by the hand. In a daze, I let my younger sister walk me out the door as if I was a child.

Outside, the ghetto was shrouded in darkness. There was no moon, and the stars seemed faint and dim. We walked hand in hand in silence on the desolate road leading to Marishin. I had the mysterious and distinct feeling that my mother was walking along with us.

We entered the work shed that had been designated as the "Straw Resort." Like always, the stagnant and suffocating air hit me as we walked in. The foul odor was a mixture of the rotten straw and the sweat of the gigantic, mindless human machine that we all had become.

We took our stand at our usual places, one opposite the other. We worked silently, each of us absorbed in our thoughts. My sister had her eyes fixed on her braid, while my eyes were fixed on her nimble fingers as she skillfully braided the straw together.

My mind was miles and miles away, so it took several moments for the significance of the damp spots on her braid of straw to sink in. I looked up sharply in time to see two more glistening tears slide off her cheek. Sarah was weeping silently, her shoulders shaking with the effort not to sob.

I felt a sudden wave of self-disgust. I had been wallowing in self-pity, reveling in the misery of knowing that I was the only one who truly mourned for my mother. How could I have been so blind? Sarah desperately needed comfort, and she needed me to give it to her.

I knew I should say something, but I couldn't get the words out of my mouth. I lowered my eyes, silently resolving to speak to Sarah on the way home.

The bell rang. We folded our braids and left the shed. Outside, the sun was just beginning to rise; we had worked the entire night-shift. Sarah and I walked home in heavy silence. I opened my mouth a dozen times, only to close it again. I didn't know what to say. I didn't know if I could speak at all, even if I tried.

The longer we walked, the more powerful our silence became. Suddenly, Sarah stopped and nudged me. I stopped walking, looking questioningly into her huge, frightened eyes. She obviously had something to say.

In a broken, shaking voice, she stammered, "Y-you have to be my mother now."

I stared at her in shock. She was trembling violently, and I suddenly realized it was even harder for Sarah than it was for me. She needed me, and wouldn't it help me as well to share my grief? I hugged her tightly, and the tears I had been holding back for so long finally came. The two of us stood together in the middle of the road, crying bitterly on each other's shoulders. Then, slowly, we started walking home again, hand in hand.

It was only then that I realized that I had been wearing Mammeshe's coat all night.

That breakthrough was only a beginning. It didn't take me long to slip back into depression. Part of my drive to survive the ghetto had been my mother's need for me, but now I felt like there was no purpose to living any more.

Once, Chaya Rochwerger literally dragged me out of the apartment. She found me lying on the floor, dirty and despondent. She picked me up bodily and stood me on my feet, brushing off my skirt.

"Why don't you just leave me alone?" I begged her. "I don't want to go anywhere."

"Chanka!" she insisted. "Fayga Zelicka is giving a *shiur* today. You don't want to miss that." Chaya ignored all my protests and manhandled me out the door.

A heavy falling snow covered the ground. It was a long way from our apartment to Fayga's house. Chaya walked briskly, pulling me along as I stumbled and dragged my feet. As we neared Fayga's house, though, I felt a faint spark of interest. Fayga's *shiurim* were always interesting. She was one of the last former leaders of Bnos to remain in the ghetto. Nearly all the others had already been deported.

By the time we arrived, the place was already crowded. The girls were sitting around a small table, two girls squeezed onto each chair. Some were even sitting on the floor. We exchanged quiet nods; nobody seemed to feel like talking. Then Fayga stood up and began to speak.

It was completely quiet when Fayga was lecturing. Halfway through the *shiur*, she paused for a few moments so that the girls could switch places and let those sitting on the floor have a chance to sit on the chairs.

The room was very cold, like every room in the ghetto. We sat closely together, trying to warm each other. But even though our limbs were freezing, we all felt a warm glow inside. Fayga's words transported us from the world of the ghetto, a world of misery, fear and death, to a world of beauty and justice.

Chaya and I walked home together. I couldn't thank her, but she squeezed my arm tightly, and I knew she understood.

It was Tatteshe, though, who finally broke through the thick shell in which I was hiding. He was very concerned about me. He had lost his wife, and he didn't want to lose his oldest daughter, too. He wanted to force me to fight for my survival, instead of just giving up and sitting down to die.

He seemed infinitely patient, sitting silently by while I stormed and raved and railed against the unfairness of it all. He spoke quietly to me, sneaking words of calm and strength past the barriers I had so stubbornly erected. Slowly, the barriers came down.

My father and I spoke about my mother whenever we could. He was really the one who managed to keep me holding on to my sanity. We both slowly healed together as he taught me to remember what I had lost, but to appreciate what I still had at the same time.

# CHAPTER 15

■

## Disintegration of a Family

THANKS TO MY FATHER, I WAS GETTING BACK TO NOR-
mal. I was able to think coherently, and I regained
my determination to survive in spite of the Nazis'
intentions to kill us all. There was, however, one thing that
still troubled me. Why hadn't we heard from Binyamin? I
hadn't seen him since Mammeshe's funeral.

My father came home one day with a very pale face. I tried
to talk to him, but it took him a long time before he was able
to speak to me. It seemed that he had seen Brocha walking in
the street, and she was obviously pregnant. I understood why
my father was so frightened; pregnant women were a favorite
target for the Nazis. I offered up a silent *tefillah* that everything would be all right.

I grew more and more worried as the days passed by. I

knew there had been a particularly vicious *Aktion* in Binyamin's section of the ghetto. My father went to check things out, but he wouldn't tell me what he discovered. As time went on, however, I gradually came to understand that Brocha had been taken for deportation. I silently chalked up one more atrocity that the Germans had committed against our family.

One afternoon in the early spring, Sarah came home in a terrible state, half-choking on tears of rage and frustration. She was completely incapable of saying a word. My father and I tried to calm her down, but she was too hysterical to do anything but cry.

Trying to get control of herself, she began to tell us what she had seen. She couldn't seem to speak in sentences; her words came out in disjointed phrases, echoing her confusion and state of mind.

"Binyamin!" she choked out. "Binyamin . . . was harnessed . . . *efacalia* barrel . . ."

I felt a sudden chill. Binyamin, harnessed to an *efacalia* barrel? It couldn't be! The *efacalia* barrels were excrement containers on wheels. The excrement was taken from the latrines in the apartment houses and carried through the streets, to be dumped into ditches at the edge of the ghetto. How could Binyamin be harnessed to one of those terrible things?

"It was Binyamin," Sarah moaned, rocking herself back and forth. "His feet were dripping mud. He—he was bent over double. So cold outside—he was dripping with sweat, Binyamin, he's so sick, it's so wrong . . ."

My father could see that she was getting hysterical again. He hugged her tightly, gently wiping away the tears from her eyes.

"Sarah," he whispered, stroking her hair. "What is it that

118

bothers you? Are you humiliated that Binyamin is doing such work?"

Sarah didn't say anything, but she nodded miserably. I, too, felt unbearable shame for Binyamin, forced to do such demeaning work.

"Sarah," Tatteshe said again. "When a person starves, he dies. If working the *efacalia* barrels is the only way Binyamin can get food, then that is what he must do. Humiliation and shame are only feelings, Sarah. You can't die of feelings. Binyamin is my son, and I want him to live. I love him, too."

Sarah wept again, but more quietly. I was horrified at the picture she had presented to us. Even if I could forget the shame of it—and I wasn't sure that I could—I was afraid for Binyamin.

Working the *efacalia* barrels was very dangerous. The back-breaking work was exhausting, and the constant exposure to human waste made the *efacalia* workers very susceptible to disease. Those who worked the barrels received extra food rations, but they usually didn't last very long. Illnesses of all kinds caught up with them very quickly.

My father and I exchanged glances over Sarah's head. I nodded wordlessly and went to find Binyamin.

It took every bit of strength not to break down and cry when I finally found him. Where was the Binyamin I remembered? Where was the young man with the bounce in his step and the strength and vigor to learn until all hours of the night? Where was the older brother whose steadfast courage had always been an inspiration to me? The Binyamin standing before me was a skeleton with flaming eyes. He wasn't much more than skin and bones.

We didn't say a word to each other. Words were too narrow, too shallow to express my pain. I wrapped him in an old blanket, shuddering at how thin and gaunt he seemed. The streets were full of slush and ice, and his walk was hesitant and uncertain. I held onto him, almost carrying him as we stumbled on together. He was so light! I choked back tears as I remembered how strong and robust he had been on the day of his wedding. I ached for him, for the violent shivering that took over his entire body and for the hands that seemed burning hot to my touch. The walk to our apartment should have taken only twenty minutes, but it seemed to take forever.

My father's face turned ashen when he opened the apartment door and saw what Binyamin looked like. He gently put an arm around his son's shoulders and helped him to the table, where a glass of hot tea was waiting for him. I found myself shuddering again as I saw how Binyamin's hands trembled as he falteringly lifted the glass of tea. My father and Sarah looked as frightened and miserable as I did at the sight of Binyamin and his awful state of health. I couldn't help thinking how horrified Mammeshe would be if she could see her only son in such a terrible condition.

We put Binyamin to bed and called in Dr. Berger.

"Sit up, now . . . yes, that's right. Now breathe . . . nice and slow, please. Does that hurt? Yes? Cough, please . . . yes, and again . . . very good. All right, Binyamin, just lay back and relax. I'll be back in a moment." Dr. Berger straightened up and tucked his stethoscope into his little bag. He looked at my father and jerked his head in the direction of the door. The two men walked out of the room to speak confidentially.

I watched my father as Dr. Berger spoke to him in a whisper. His face turned pale as he listened to the doctor. Tears glittered in Tatteshe's eyes as he quietly answered Dr. Berger's questions. I was afraid to ask what was happening, because I was afraid of the possible answers.

Finally, Dr. Berger came back into Binyamin's room. He pulled up a stool and sat down next to the bed.

"Binyamin," he said, "you have tuberculosis. I know that you don't want to eat any non-kosher meat, but it is my opinion that, in this case, you must. The next time horse meat is rationed out, I want you to eat it."

Tuberculosis! I leaned against the wall for support. I knew that it could very easily be fatal.

"Are you sure that I'll recover if I eat the non-kosher meat?" Binyamin's voice, once strong and vibrant, seemed very weak to my ears.

"No, I'm not," said Dr. Berger frankly. "But, Binyamin, you're in very bad shape. You ought to do whatever you can to get better."

"If you cannot be sure that the horse meat will save my life," Binyamin said slowly, "then I'm not going to eat it. I will not poison my body with *treif*."

Dr. Berger looked resigned, almost as if he had expected such an answer. Nodding quietly at my father, he picked up his bag and walked out. Tatteshe walked over to Binyamin's bed and sat down on the stool. He lifted Binyamin's hand and held it tightly.

Tatteshe sat there for several minutes, just holding Binyamin's hand without saying anything. Then he gently touched Binyamin on the cheek and said in a low voice, "Binyamin, maybe you should reconsider?"

"No," Binyamin whispered. "I can't eat *treif*. I would choke over every bite if I tried to put it in my mouth. He can't promise that it will help me, and I can't take the chance of eating *treif* for nothing."

My father said nothing. He knew that there was no point

in arguing. He bowed his head, and I watched as his tears slowly dripped onto Binyamin's hand.

Binyamin's health deteriorated steadily. Somehow, though, his spiritual health seemed to soar to great heights. Propped up in bed, he would remain absorbed in his *Gemara* for hours at end. He feverishly wrote down his Torah thoughts on whatever scraps of paper I could bring him. He was constantly humming *chassidishe niggunim*, and his voice rang out clearly on *Shabbos* when he sang the *zemiros*. With each day, however, he grew weaker and weaker, until he didn't even have the strength to sit up anymore. When he was too weak to talk, I knew that it was the end.

Memories flashed through my mind, glimpses of the older brother I had loved so much. Binyamin playing games with me, when he was still only a child . . . all those glances we used to exchange, telling each other things without ever saying a word . . . Binyamin swaying over a *sefer,* completely oblivious to everything around him . . . walking home from *shul* with my father on Friday night, his eyes aglow with the *kedushah* of *Shabbos* . . . Binyamin's *seudah* in the ghetto with all his friends . . . dancing at his own wedding, alive with joy in the midst of death . . . patiently teaching me how to be steadfast in my *emunah* . . . singing *zemiros* in that beautiful, haunting voice . . . reciting *Kaddish* for Mammeshe, that beautiful voice choked with tears . . . His *hasmodah.* His wonderful nature. His strong *bitachon* in *Hashem.* His kindness and warmth . . . Binyamin. Binyamin Landman, who was dying of tuberculosis.

I stood silently by as Binyamin mouthed the words of *Viduy.* Then I turned away. Sarah and I walked down the stairs and stood in the courtyard, staring at nothing. We couldn't bear to watch as our twenty-one year old brother died.

Like all other people in the world, I thought bitterly, we had once been a happy, loving family, with a home where we lived in peace. Now we lived in a miserable hovel in the ghetto, and we had gone from five to three. My mother was gone. My brother was dead. I felt as if my life was hanging on a rope that was steadily fraying to shreds. It wouldn't take long for the rope to snap completely, and then I, too, would follow in the footsteps of Mammeshe and Binyamin.

Once again, it was my father who managed to get past my depression and keep me going. The three of us were living like hunted animals, concentrating on simply surviving for yet another day. By day we were plagued with suffering and fear; we spent our sleepness nights trying to ignore the torture of constant hunger. Throughout all our troubles, Tatteshe remained as firm as a rock. His strength of belief was a great source of encouragement. His very presence was a comfort, and I felt safe as long as I knew that he was nearby. Strangely enough, Sarah and I were never listed for deportation. I was deeply convinced that my father was somehow protecting us from being sent to our deaths.

# BOOK THREE

———————— ■ ————————

# The Fury
of the
Storm

# CHAPTER 16

---■---

# The Mice Are Caught

ONDITIONS IN THE GHETTO WENT FROM TERRIBLE TO impossible. Rumkowski kept repeating his tiresome litany—anyone who was deported was being sent to work somewhere else, and the only way to avoid death was to work hard and please the Germans. Nobody believed him any more. They promised a loaf of bread to anyone who chose to be deported, but nobody was tempted. We all felt that starvation and suffering was better than death.

The *Aktions* began to occur with increasing frequency. Not only were there countless roundups, but the lists of people that were to be deported increased every day. The resorts where we worked were liquidated, and everyone that had produced goods for the Germans was put on the deportation list. Somehow, my father managed to get Sarah and me off the list, saving us from the dreaded *Aktion* and certain death.

We all knew, though, that it was just a delaying tactic. It was 1944, and it was very clear that the entire ghetto was going to be liquidated. People tried to go into hiding, but without much success.

One thing that I remember in particular is how people desperately tried to hold on to the illusion that if we kept producing goods for the Germans, we would be safe. "Work is our passport to life," as Rumkowski used to say. Sarah and I had been working in the gardens of Marishin, and our jobs had been cancelled. Our director sent us out to cut the high grass in the cemetery and gather the grass into bundles. It was a senseless job. The whole point was simply to keep us employed.

It was eerie to stand among the dozens of freshly covered graves. There wasn't a single person on our work-detail who did not have several members of their family buried there. How many times had I walked into a house to visit a friend, only to find it empty of life? Sometimes, the door was swinging crazily on its hinges, and signs of a scuffle pointed towards an *Aktion*. Once or twice I had found a silent figure lying on the floor, covered with a white sheet. There weren't even enough of us living to bury all our dead. I stood among the graves, the grass swaying in the soft breeze, and I found myself wondering how long it would be before we took our places among the dead.

A gentle touch on my arm snapped me out of my reverie. Sarah was looking at me anxiously, wondering what was wrong. I smiled at her, assuring her that everything was fine. And that, of course, was my reason for staying alive: Sarah. Sarah needed me. As long as there was someone depending on me, I would do my best to make sure that I wouldn't let her down.

We had been playing a cat and mouse game lately. When an *Aktion* approached our neighborhood, we would flee to an area where the *Aktion* had already taken place. We were constantly trying to stay a step ahead of the Nazis, but we knew that eventually we would be caught.

One day, my father took me aside to speak to me privately. "You realize, Chanka, that there's no way of stopping the liquidation of the entire ghetto."

I nodded, not trusting myself to speak.

Tatteshe sighed and looked down at his hands. "We might not be able to stay together. I'll do my best to stay with you and Sarah, but it might not be possible. If we get separated, we will need some kind of sign so that we can find each other again." He paused, rubbing his eyes with weariness. "We will combine our last name and your mother's maiden name. That will be our sign—not Landman or Lerner, but Landlerner. That way, you will know that anyone using that name has had direct contact with me. I hope this will all be unnecessary, but it pays to be prepared."

"Yes, Tatteshe," I said softly. I didn't want to ask him what would happen if none of us managed to survive.

Slowly, I began to pack our few remaining possessions into a valise. My father, who was usually very particular and orderly, was frighteningly indifferent to my packing.

"We're not going to need that," he said every time I placed another item into the valise. "There's no point in all this packing. The Germans won't let us keep anything, anyway."

Finally, he just walked out of the room. I didn't understand why he was acting like that, and it made me very nervous. Then I stopped for a moment. Where was it written that only I could get nervous, upset or depressed? Sarah and I demanded so much from Tatteshe—what did we give him in return? I resolved to be more understanding of my father's feelings in the future.

Unfortunately, I didn't have the chance to carry out my resolution.

We had spent the day dodging another *Aktion,* but the night had been wonderfully quiet. We returned to the apartment for the first good night's sleep in weeks. The next morning, it was still relatively quiet, so I decided we would have time to sit down to a decent meal.

Of course, "decent" is a relative term. Our total food supply at that point consisted of three beets. Still, considering the usual ghetto fare, three beets cooked into a soup would make a perfectly good meal.

Sarah came into the room as I was grating the beets into some hot water. She looked into the pot and sniffed appreciatively, then offered to go outside and make sure that there were no Germans anywhere in sight.

"We might as well make sure that we can eat in peace," she pointed out. "I don't hear any trucks, so it must be pretty safe. I'll just take a quick look to make sure that there are no SS men around, and then we can all sit down and enjoy your beet soup."

Through the window I saw her cross the street and look around. Sarah took a few steps forward toward the chestnut tree at the corner of our block. Suddenly, I saw a young man walking toward her, a pleasant smile on his face. He was bareheaded, his hair moving gently in the breeze.

Alarmed, I started toward the window, opening my mouth to call out to Sarah. With shocking quickness, two dogs almost as big as Sarah herself pounced on her, barking furiously. Screaming with terror, Sarah tried to run back into the apartment, but the dogs had their teeth firmly fastened in her skirt and followed her into the apartment. The young man, his smile abruptly hardened into the grim smirk typical of all the Nazis, was only a step behind.

Sarah was still screaming with panic as the dogs jumped on top of her. I backed away in terror. The pot overturned, and hot water spilled all over the floor. The dogs attacked all three of us, snarling horribly and ripping at our clothes. The SS man, who had been watching the entire scene with evident enjoyment, hefted his rifle and began to club my father over the head with casual efficiency.

"*Raus, raus! Alle raus!* Out, out! Everyone out!" The Nazi gestured in the direction of the door. Shoving Tatteshe with his rifle, the German checked to see that the dogs were making sure that Sarah and I were following. I have no idea how I managed to think coherently under the circumstances, but I grabbed the valise, as well as a knapsack I had prepared for Sarah, before following the German out the door.

A long line of trucks and wagons were winding their way toward us. Men, women and children were crammed into the trucks and wagons, guarded by SS men armed with machine guns. The sky was gray and dreary in the early autumn morning, and the weather seemed to reflect our despair. There were no screams, no pleas for mercy. Everyone seemed resigned, as if they had known that there was no avoiding this final deportation.

For some reason, the three of us were not shoved onto the trucks. Instead, we had the honor of being escorted on foot by our very own personal Nazi. With the dogs snapping at our heels, we walked to Czarnieckiego, the deportation center.

Czarnieckiego was full of Jews, as bewildered and lost as
we were. Nobody knew what was going to happen, although
we all suspected that it wasn't going to be very pleasant. My
father, Sarah and I joined the others sitting on the asphalt
floor. Families huddled together, desperate not to be separated. We were each given a loaf of bread, but I was suspicious. The Nazis were trying to kill us, weren't they? I was
afraid that the bread was poisoned, and I didn't want to eat.
So much for the generous loaf of bread at transport, I
thought wryly.

As the shadows lengthened, we were all bullied onto a
train. We were sealed in a windowless cattle car, stuffy with
lack of fresh air. It became chokingly hot, and there was
hardly any air to breathe. I hoped that when the train started
moving some air would filter in.

It seemed like hours before we finally started moving, and
it was no comfort when we did. The stench from sweat, vomit
and human bodies crushed together was suffocating. Children wailed, begging their mothers to take away the pain.
Women cried out to the world in general, asking for mercy
on their children. Nobody could do anything to help at all.

We were all standing in the car, body pressed against
body, like sardines in a can. Here and there people were
actually piled on top of each other. Some parents had their
children on their shoulders, trying to keep them above the
general crush. Others took turns supporting each other,
trying to reserve their energy.

For more than twenty-four hours we travelled in those
horrible conditions. The moaning, screaming and crying of
the sick and the children tore at my insides like a physical
pain. The suffering I witnessed was absolutely shattering. I
felt as if I was slowly losing my mind, and I watched with

morbid fascination as a young girl leaning against the wall of the train slowly pulled her hair out, strand by strand.

Suddenly, in the midst of all the chaos and confusion, a single sweet voice rose above the cries and screams.

"*Ani maamin, ani maamin, be'emunah sheleimah . . .*" It was Tatteshe, singing an old, haunting melody. "I believe, I believe with perfect faith in the coming of *Mashiach . . .*" The song had an almost magical effect on all of us. The entire crowd fell silent; then several of the men picked up the tune, tears streaming down their cheeks as they sang the words that proclaimed that a Jew always believes that we will be redeemed from our exile. I, too, had to blink away my tears as I watched the awesome spectacle.

Several men slowly donned their *taleisim* and joined my father in prayer. Even here in the cattle car, Tatteshe managed to find a *minyan!* I thought back to the time when Binyamin had pointed out that suffering was nothing new to the Jewish nation. With all the changes in the world, and all the centuries that had gone by, the situation for the Jews is always the same. I watched the men *daven,* and I found comfort in the knowledge that I was, after all, a link in the chain—a chain of suffering and a chain of survival.

# CHAPTER 17

■

# Welcome to Auschwitz

W E HAD BEEN TRAVELLING FOR HOURS AND HOURS, and I had completely lost track of time. It was with a tired feeling of surprise that I realized that the train was finally slowing down. We were approaching our destination, but what was it?

A strident whistle sounded as we groaned to a stop. There was a last moment of silence, as if everyone was holding their breath, then the sealed doors slid open with a deafening bang, and we were thrown headlong into the hellish nightmare of life in Auschwitz.

A group of SS men armed with guns and whips ordered us all out of the cattle car. We were all stiff and sore from the long, agonizing train ride, but the kicks and punches we received were more than enough of an incentive. We tried to stumble out of the car, falling over our own feet, but many of us were exhausted from the trip and unable to move. We were shoved down like bags of garbage. Those who could not jump out of the car fast enough were rolled or pulled out. Anyone who resisted or wasn't quick enough to comply was dragged away or thrown aside. In minutes, the ground was covered with human bodies.

The rest of us were quickly lined up next to the trains, five people per row. The Nazis waved their rifles and marched us along a rough, gravelly road. After the long train ride, the march seemed endless.

My nose twitched as I gradually became aware of a strange, repellent smell. I craned my neck, trying to see ahead and discover what was causing that horrible stench. All I could see was thick, ugly smoke surging upward in the bitter breeze.

"This is the smell of burning bodies," someone said in a hoarse whisper.

I don't know how that person knew, but I could tell that he was right. The smoke looked uglier, more vicious somehow. Some of the women were weeping softly, and I was surprised to feel tears on my own cheeks. I wondered vaguely how soon it would be before I, too, would disappear in a stinking cloud of smoke, never to be seen again.

I felt a hand grip my arm. I looked down and saw that Sarah was holding on to me. I squeezed back tightly. Neither of us said a word.

The line came to an abrupt halt. Up ahead, I could see that we were being divided into two groups.

There was a man standing at the head of the line, sweeping his gaze over each person with the same casual scrutiny. Anyone who looked too old or sick to work was met

135

with a jerk of the thumb, pointing to the left. Mothers with young children clinging tightly to their skirts were pointed in the same direction. They were hurried along with shouts, kicks and rifle butts. Other people, mostly those who looked basically healthy, were gestured towards the right.

The process of selection was done in the most gruesome and heartless manner. Children were torn from their mothers, and if a mother protested or tried to get her baby back, an SS man shot them both. People that tried to cross from one column to another were killed for their pains. After all, they were disrupting the entire process! The Germans wanted the whole thing to go quickly and smoothly, and they had no patience for anything that would create any delays.

The left column was quickly led away. At the time, I had no idea what the whole thing meant. I didn't know that the man, who looked relaxed and almost bored, was the infamous Dr. Mengele. I didn't know that we were only a few hundred yards from the gas chambers and crematoriums, and I didn't know that the left column was slated for death.

Those of us that were in the right column had a few moments to look around. Everywhere I looked, I saw the dead bodies of old people and tiny babies. Some of the babies were covered with the bodies of their dead mothers, lying in the same position in which they had been shot as they tried to protect their children. I remember in particular one small leg in a white sock and black patent-leather shoe sticking out from underneath a woman's corpse. Only a few feet away from the dead mother and child, a young boy was sprawled over the body of his dead father, still twitching in the last agonies of death.

The soldiers began to separate men from women. Sarah and I, clinging tightly to each other in fright, were half-whimpering with terror. I held on to Sarah's hand tightly, afraid to let go. What if we got separated too?

As the SS man ordered my father to move, he hesitated. He started to say something to me, but the Nazi thrust his rifle butt into my father's back with such force that he almost fell to the ground as he was propelled in the direction of the men's column. When he regained his balance, he looked across to the women's column, seeking out Sarah and me. He saw us, and our eyes met for an endless moment. I felt as if his eyes were speaking to me, urging me to be calm and to have faith in Hashem. Then the men behind him pushed Tatteshe roughly ahead, and I lost sight of him completely.

Sarah and I continued to hold hands as we stumbled along in our column. I had the sick, sinking feeling that I would never see my father again, and all I could concentrate on was not losing Sarah, too.

As we made our way along the rocky path, one of my shoes came off. I turned to pick it up, but Sarah grabbed my arm and pulled me violently ahead. As I lurched after her, a shot rang out. I watched, stunned, as a man tumbled to the ground only a few feet away. I recognized him; he was one of the men who had been praying with my father in the cattle car. I couldn't shake off the horrible feeling that he had taken a bullet that was meant for me.

I didn't look back anymore. This was not a place where I could look back, or do anything else, with any kind of safety. The only thing to do was blindly follow orders. Sarah gripped my hand more tightly, as if she sensed my inner trembling. I squeezed her hand back, and we just kept going.

I wondered if it would be possible to escape. There were so many of us; how could the Nazis possibly keep track? Couldn't it be possible for some of us to sneak away? I was shocked out of my fantasy by a vicious dog jumping on me. I shied away in panic, only to realize that the line had moved ahead already. I hurried after the slowly moving column, abandoning all thoughts of escape. This was Auschwitz, and I was slowly coming to realize that we wouldn't even be able to call our bodies our own.

The woman walking in front of me was crying and pulling out her hair. The entire column of women seemed to be weeping. The cries and shouts were, for the most part, indistinct, but I was startled to hear a sudden scream from a girl standing only a few feet away. "Smoke! Smell!" she shrieked. I had no idea what she was talking about, but everyone seemed to pick up the cry. Screams and wails rang out in the air. I heard someone shouting, "Shades, soap! The smoke brings the smell!" I had no idea what it meant. It was only later that I found out that the human body was exploited to the utmost in Auschwitz; once all the strength had been used up, the body was used with complete efficiency. The skin was used for lamp shades and pocketbooks, the fat was used for soap, and even the ashes were used to fertilize German soil. At the time, however, all I knew was that the shouts and screams were frightening and unnerving.

All the years in the darkness of the Lodz Ghetto, I had felt that death would not touch me because my father protected me. Now he was gone, lost somewhere in the mass of human bodies milling around in confusion. I wished with all my might that he was here to calm me down with his wisdom and inner strength.

We reached an intersection in the road, and the rifle butts and kicks indicated that we were supposed to turn left. I noticed with surprise that there was money scattered all over the sand—German marks, Polish zlotys and American dollars.

Gold watches and silver candlesticks also littered the ground, only inches away from the bodies that were sprawled all over the earth. The Germans were stripping us of all our material wealth before committing us to the gas chambers.

I watched a man gasp his last breath before his head dropped to the sand. A young boy was crying over his father's body, only to be hauled away by the collar and thrown back into line. There were dead and dying all around me. It looked like a slaughterhouse.

Maybe this is all a dream, I thought confusedly. Maybe it's just a horrible nightmare, and I'll wake up. A sharp blow on my head and shoulder told me that it wasn't a dream. This was Auschwitz, and this was our reality: a world of smoke and fire, of ashes and gas, a universe of madness where death was king.

I was alarmed to see that my father's column had disappeared. I was frantically desperate to keep my father in sight, but the entire left column had been taken elsewhere. Now, with the left column out of the way, the Germans were walking up and down the rows, looking for twins.

Most of us thought that twins would be getting special treatment. Perhaps they would get better bunks, decent hygienic conditions, permission to keep their own clothing and even better rations. Two girls standing nearby were whispering to each other; they were cousins, but they looked alike and could easily pass for twins. They stepped forward to join the new group. Individual twins also came forward of their own free will. Perhaps it was because the new group was formed on the right, and we were already becoming conditioned to think that "right" meant life. At any rate, Sarah and I were disappointed that we looked too different to join the group of twins and get preferred treatment.

Our disappointment only lasted until the next morning.

We found out that the special group of twins was sent over to the Gypsy Camp, where horribly obscene experiments were performed on them. Most of the experiments resulted in the death of the victims.

As the "lucky" group of twins was led away, I began to take in my surroundings. There seemed to be hundreds and hundreds of barracks, forming a rectangular network of streets as far as the eye could see. I felt queasy at the idea that so many people were interned in the camp.

Those of us that were remaining were led off to our blocks of barracks, where we would be shaven, showered, and clothed with a "new" disinfected dress and wooden clogs. Part of the long human snake of people, I blindly followed orders, eventually ending up in a barracks packed with other girls. The barracks were narrow—only five people could stand next to each other, and it was a very tight squeeze—but it seemed endlessly long.

As I entered the barracks, a Nazi woman grabbed me by the hair and yanked me towards her.

"Where's the ring?" she snarled at me. "Where did you hide it?"

"I don't have a ring," I gasped, tears of pain coming to my eyes.

"Your mother's ring!" she hissed. "Where did you hide the diamond?"

"My mother is dead," I choked out. "She died two years ago. I sold her diamond ring to pay the doctor. See, these are her clothes, I don't have anything, anything . . ." By this point I was crying, begging her to leave me alone. I felt as if I was going out of my mind. Her face, her smell, her breath assaulted my senses. Suddenly, she ripped my mouth open, nearly knocking me over in her viciousness.

"No golden teeth, hey?" She spat on me and shoved me ahead on top of another girl, who was crying softly. By this point, I was also crying, just like everybody else.

There were four people standing next to me; I couldn't even tell if they were girls or women. They all looked alike, because their heads were shaved. There was no way to distinguish their age. It was only when I looked at them and touched my own head that I realized that I had no hair. My head was clean shaven. When did they shave it? Who shaved it? And where was I when they shaved it?

Oh, Tatteshe, Tatteshe, where are you? Are they treating you like this, too? People were being horribly abused wherever I looked. I longed to see my father, to hear his words of comfort and see his warming smile. But he was somewhere in a barracks just like this one, and he was probably suffering the same way I was.

We were all jammed against the right wall, leaving a narrow aisle on the left just wide enough for one person to get by. The people that were shaving the girls moved freely back and forth, clobbering with their truncheons anyone who dared to even breathe too deeply. Anyone who cried out loud, stepped out of line or protested was beaten mercilessly. I was horrified to find out that these people weren't even Nazis; they were *kapos*, inmates chosen by the Germans to do the job. Some of them might even be Jews! How could they treat their people like this?

There were some tiny windows on the left side. When the *kapo* wasn't watching, I moved over to a window and peered out, trying to catch a glimpse of what was happening outside. Across the sandy yard there was another barracks, with similar windows facing me. I tried to see into the other barracks to find out if everyone else was being treated the same horrible way we were.

Suddenly, I saw a man poke his head out of one of the windows. He, too, was looking around outside the barracks. When he turned his face in my direction, I immediately recognized him, and an incredulous joy flooded my entire being.

"Tatteshe! Tatteshe! I am here!" I shrieked at the top of my voice. "Tatteshe! Can you see me?"

A rubber truncheon instantly crashed down on my head, followed by a torrent of blows all over my body. The *kapo* viciously tore me away from the place where I saw my beloved father for the last time.

After a few kicks for good measure, the *kapo* shoved me backwards and nearly sent me sprawling. I crashed into the person standing behind me, and I would have fallen if the person would not have held me up.

I'm in a world of monkeys, I thought with disbelief. For a moment I couldn't make out the connection between me and the little monkey boy standing next to me, anxiously peering into my face. It was only when the little creature burst into tears that I recognized poor Sarah. If I had seen her in the street, I would have walked away from her without giving her a second glance.

So ended my first day of initiation in the death camp of Auschwitz.

# CHAPTER 18

## The Endless Nightmare

WE WERE LED VIA KICKS, BLOWS AND CURSES TO OUR block in "C" camp. By the time we reached Block Twenty-Five, night had already fallen. We stared in dismay at the barracks. It was an empty building with no windows and a damp, muddy asphalt floor. This was to be our home for as long as we survived the selections.

We were met by our *blokowa*, the woman in charge of our barracks, who ordered us to go to sleep. We stared at her in disbelief. Sleep? There was barely room for all of us to stand, much less to lie down! With a supercilious sneer, the *blokowa* showed us what to do.

One girl sat on the floor and spread her feet apart. Another girl literally sat in her lap, spreading her legs apart for the next girl. We were crammed together so tightly that we were pinned into place, unable to move our legs or bodies. We were twenty-five hundred girls, packed into a small barracks building.

The first and the last in a row were the worst off. The first didn't have anyone to lean on, and she had to support the weight of the entire row. The last girl in the row didn't have anybody on her lap, but she was usually the first one to get beaten, stepped on and walked over. When a *kapo* wanted to hit any of us, she just stepped on the last girl and struck her. No one was in a comfortable position, but I was relieved not to suffer the additional torture of being the first or last in a row.

When we had been arranged to the *blokowa's* satisfaction, she told us that we would be spending the night in our current positions and that we should all be quiet and go to sleep.

Silence fell. It was pitch dark in the barracks, and no one spoke. The few girls who had tried to whisper encouragement to each other had been given a taste of the *blokowa's* rubber truncheon, and none of us wanted to get the same treatment. I tried to fall asleep, wistfully thinking that maybe I would wake up in the morning to discover that the whole thing was only a bad nightmare.

Absorbed in my thinking, I was surprised to feel a hand groping along the left side of my body. Alarmed and more than a little uncomfortable, I realized that it must be the girl pressed against me. I tried to move away from her, but I couldn't even shift my weight towards the right side. I didn't understand what she could possibly want from me until she tried to reach under my arm. She was reaching for my bread! Somehow, I had held onto that piece of bread distributed at the deportation center in Lodz, a lifetime ago. Had it really been only this morning? Throughout all the confusion and terror, that piece of bread had remained clenched tightly in my fist. Now the girl was trying to reach the bread and take it for herself.

I found out later that the girl had lost her mind when she witnessed the murder of her parents. Actually, an attempt to steal bread was as rare in Auschwitz as a Nazi with a kind heart. Again and again, I saw women handing their bread rations to friends when they thought they were going to their deaths, only to have the bread returned to them untouched when they miraculously returned to the barracks. Selflessness and generosity were the norm among the inmates. The girl trying to steal my bread was certainly out of the ordinary.

I wanted to scream at her, but I was afraid of the *blokowa* and her ever-ready truncheon. I squeezed my hand tightly, refusing to give in to her. She clawed at my back with her sharp nails, trying to force me to give her my bread. I didn't get any sleep that night, but I had the bread to share with Sarah in the morning.

It was still dark when a shrill whistle sounded. With kicks and curses, the *blokowa* ordered us to get up for the *appell,* or roll call. We began our second day in Auschwitz in a haze of sorrow, depression and confusion. The *blokowa* had no patience for our misery. She let us know in no uncertain terms exactly what we could expect in the future.

"You didn't come here to live, you pigs!" she yelled in a shrill, spiteful voice. "You came here to die. Now go outside and see how your sisters and brothers go up to heaven in smoke! You'll follow them soon!"

Auschwitz was designed to destroy us, body and soul. We suffered from overcrowding, dirt, stench, hunger and thirst. Everything that could possibly be used as torture was applied with relish and enthusiasm.

Water was so scarce that washing was simply out of the question. What little water they gave us was polluted and of a sickening dark yellow color. We drank the water out of necessity, closing our eyes to the color and smell.

The food seemed to burn us up from the inside, leaving us weak and drained. Instead of nourishing us, the food made us sick. Most of us ended up contracting dysentery.

There was one latrine for thirty thousand women, a single deep ditch with several planks straddling the gap. We were only allowed to use it once a day, which was a torment for those of us suffering from dysentery. The stench was unbearable; we were never allowed to change our clothing or given paper with which to clean ourselves.

We were forced to stand on *appell* for hours and hours at end. Sometimes they wanted to count us, sometimes they wanted to make a selection, and sometimes they simply wanted to make us suffer. Punishments were administered at whim; we were often forced to stand at attention for no reason at all. If a girl was missing, thousands of women would end up kneeling for hours until she was found. The strain of remaining motionless for such a long time was one of the most exquisite tortures of all.

The most frightening type of *appell* was when Dr. Mengele stood at the front of the line to make a selection. Any girl who seemed weak risked a final trip to the gas chambers and crematoria. Sometimes, Mengele would select a girl for death simply because he didn't like her face.

Most girls that were selected went to the gas chambers with resignation; they were either too indifferent or too stunned to resist. There was also the overwhelming fear that lurked at the back of everyone's mind: resistance could cause not only the death of the girl that fought back but also the deaths of everyone standing nearby. How could we fight when we knew that others would suffer because of us?

The *kapos* and the *blokowas* treated us as cruelly as possible. We were abused and beaten whenever it struck their fancy. Food rations were confiscated for the smallest infringement of the rules. Sticks and truncheons saw continual use, and the obvious enjoyment our tormentors derived from our suffering made everything seem ten times worse.

I didn't understand how the *kapos* and *blokowas* could be so cruel and unfeeling. Weren't they prisoners, too? Where was their mercy, their sense of shame? It was during one of the torturous *appells* that it finally hit me. The *kapos* were victims of the Nazis, even more than we were. Hitler had accomplished his aim of turning them into animals, just as he was trying to do with us. They had lost their compassion and relinquished their humanity, and for all that we suffered from them, they were truly the greater victims of Nazi Germany. We were still human beings with human values, while they were bestial, sadistic creatures that gloried in death.

There were times when suicide seemed an almost attractive prospect in comparison to the torment of living. The high-voltage wire fence that surrounded us seemed to call to us enticingly, urging us to end all the misery in one short burst of electricity. That was the point, of course. The Germans *wanted* to drive us to suicide. Every Jew that killed himself was one less Jew the Germans would have to murder. However, there were times when the current wasn't strong enough to kill immediately. When this happened, the victims remained hanging on the wires for days, suffering unimaginable tortures until a merciful guard shot them.

I remember when Tola Rzerker came to me in a panic.

She was a little girl, only twelve years old. She and her mother had come into Auschwitz together. They shared a *pritch*, or bunk, and they endured the *appells* side by side. Her mother had been depressed for several days, and now she had disappeared! Little Tola came to me because she had known me before the war. She wanted me to help her find her mother.

I was afraid to tell her that depressed people who disappeared usually could be found on the electrified fences. I talked around it for several minutes before the possibility dawned on her. I expected her to go into hysterics, but she didn't. Children grow up very quickly in Auschwitz.

"Chanka, will you help me look?" she whispered.

The two of us walked slowly around the perimeter of the camp. I felt sick as I forced myself to take a good look at the blackened faces of the women who had chosen suicide over the living death of Auschwitz. Spines arching backwards in a final burst of agony. Heads thrown back, stiffened in a frozen grimace of suffering. Hands clenched tightly into fists, the fingers rigid claws that would never lose their rigidity. This was the death these women had chosen. Little Tola's face grew whiter and whiter as we walked past the bodies still hanging on the fence.

Near the gate, several Nazis wearing insulated clothing were busy pulling dead bodies off the fence and flinging them with callous indifference to the ground. We edged forward, trying to avoid their attention. Tola pointed wordlessly at one of the bodies, sprawled on the ground in a grotesque splay of limbs. I motioned for her to stay back. I didn't want her to see it. She shook her head stubbornly, and as soon as the Nazis left, she ran forward and dropped down to the ground beside the pitiful corpse. I followed behind her, and even with the

148

frozen mask of death obscuring her features, I had no trouble recognizing Mrs. Rzerker.

Tola bowed her head over the body and wept. I sat on the ground next to her, holding her hand. There was nothing I could say to comfort the little girl whose mother was gone.

Sarah and I had survived for three entire days in Auschwitz, and we were still in Block Twenty-Five. It was unquestioningly the worst block in the entire camp, more crowded than any block, and the *blokowa's* sadism seemed to increase in proportion.

Late in the evening, one girl started to cry. Our *blokowa* shouted at her to be quiet, but the girl was unable to calm down, and her sobs only increased. The *blokowa* furiously grabbed a board and started hitting the girl with it. The girl's sister darted forward and tried to protect her.

The *blokowa* lowered the board and regarded the two girls with cold, glittering eyes.

"Kneel on the floor," she said to them in a deceptively quiet voice. "Kneel on the floor, and bend over."

The two girls obeyed her, while the rest of us watched with horrified fascination. We all knew what was coming, and there was nothing we could do about it.

The *blokowa* beat the two girls with her truncheon until they were coughing up blood. It was a terrible sight, made even worse by the knowledge that there was no need for her to be so vicious. There were no Nazis around; she wasn't being forced to be so brutal. She was acting so bestially because it had simply become part of her nature, part of the horror of Auschwitz.

A few hours later, I overheard a discussion between two *kapos* about a transfer of one hundred girls from Block Twenty-Five to a different block. I listened carefully, but they didn't mention why the transport was being made. For all I knew, they were simply sending one hundred girls to the gas chambers so that the block wouldn't be so crowded. I decided, however, that the risk was worth it. I beckoned to Sarah and whispered that we would volunteer to be part of the transfer when the announcement came. I could see Sarah's mind running through the same options as I had. Was leaving Block Twenty-Five worth the danger of volunteering for an unknown purpose?

We didn't have time to discuss it. As the two of us stood together, the *kapos* announced that they needed one hundred girls. Sarah and I silently stepped forward, and we were taken away.

We marched away from Block Twenty-Five. The first thing I noted was that we were not heading in the direction of the crematoria, and I breathed a sigh of relief. We were led to Block Thirty-One, which was to be our new home in Auschwitz.

The conditions in Block Thirty-One were marginally better than those in Block Twenty-Five. Instead of lying on the floor and sitting on top of each other, Block Thirty-One had crude *pritches* that were little more than slabs of wood in tiers of five. The girls lay next to each other, two to a board. I was happy to be spared the agony of human bodies pressed tightly against me from all sides.

As I lay on my *pritch* that night, I couldn't help but think how low we had sunk. A week ago, I would not have considered sleeping on a board to be practically living in the lap of luxury. Still, it was definitely a vast improvement. I said *Shema* quietly and slowly drifted off to sleep.

The next morning, we discovered that Block Twenty-Five had been liquidated in the middle of the night. Not a single girl had survived. Sarah and I looked at each other in shock and horror. If we had not given in to the impulse to get away from the block, we both would have been killed. I squeezed her hand tightly as I whispered a *tefillah* of thanks. Once again, Sarah and I had managed to survive. Perhaps we would live to see the end of the nightmare after all.

# CHAPTER 19

■

## Diversions

OMEHOW, IN THE MIDST OF ALL THE HORRORS OF Auschwitz, a small flicker of light persisted. Friends and family grew closer together, often risking their lives for the sake of one another. United against a common enemy, we bore witness time and again to the complete selflessness and dedication that only a Jew can possess.

Rachel and Rena, two of the girls sharing the *pritch* with Sarah and me, had known each other before coming to Auschwitz. Rachel was very ill, and Rena was constantly encouraging her to keep going. As time went on, however, Rachel became so sick that she was ready to give up. She told Rena that she was going to the *revier*, the camp hospital, for help.

Rena was horrified. "Please don't do that, Rachel!" she

whispered. "You know that the *revier* is just a shortcut to the gas chambers. Stay here, and I'll make sure you get better."

"I'm dying, Rena," Rachel groaned. "I'll either die of disease or die in the gas chambers. What's the point of going on?"

Rena's eyes were swimming with tears. "Rachel, you can't give up now!" she begged. "The war is almost over. We'll survive together. You have to fight, Rachel! Please, please fight back! I-I can't go on without you . . ."

Rachel pleaded with her to leave her alone, to let her die in peace, but Rena ignored her. She "organized" hot water for Rachel, arranging to sneak into the kitchens and sneak out with a bit of warm liquid every day. She lovingly nursed Rachel back to health, and both of them survived the war.

Another friend of mine named Rochel had a slightly similar story. She, too, became very sick; she had suffered from a kidney condition in Lodz, and the situation in Auschwitz only made things worse. It reached the point where her fever was so high that she could barely see straight, and she finally decided to risk going to the *revier.*

Handing her portion of bread to her little sister, she told her, "Listen, Chayale, I'm going to the *revier.* Don't try to stop me! I'd rather risk death in the gas chambers than go through this any more. I can't take it! The pain is driving me out of my mind! Maybe I can just stay there for a few days and get better."

Over Chayale's protests, Rochel left her barracks and headed for the *revier.*

Rochel took one look at the patients lying in the *revier* and begged the nurse to let her stay. Luxury of luxuries! The patients were lying on wooden planks instead of a damp asphalt floor! It was more than Rochel could bear. She pleaded with the nurse, asking her to let her rest for just a few days before returning to her barracks.

The nurse eyed Rochel and took her temperature. When the nurse read the thermometer, she was shocked at how high Rochel's fever was and agreed to let her stay. Rochel almost sobbed with relief as she tottered towards one of the wooden planks to lie down.

Just then, a young woman walked through the door. Her name was Tyla Rynder, and she grasped the situation instantly. She grabbed Rochel roughly by the arm.

"Get out of here!" she shouted. "You're too young to die!"

She propelled Rochel out the door and shoved her in the direction of her barracks. Rochel, who could hardly stand, tried to get back into the *revier,* but Tyla barred her way.

"Get back to your barracks!" she screamed. "There are enough human bodies in the ovens! Run away, quickly!"

Poor Rochel staggered back to her barracks on trembling legs. Chayale, who was overwhelmed with relief to see her back safely, plied her with questions.

"Why didn't you go? Oh, I'm so glad you didn't go! What happened?"

"Tyla Rynder wouldn't let me stay," Rochel mumbled in despair.

Later that day, Chayale came rushing into the barracks.

"Rochel!" she whispered. "Rochel, do you know what happened? Five minutes after you came back from the *revier,* they did a selection and took all the patients away!"

Rochel closed her eyes and whispered a prayer of thanks.

I never actually met Tyla myself, but I often heard her name being spoken in tones of awe and respect. She risked her life again and again for the sake of others, saving dozens of girls from the gas chambers. She stole files out of the offices, erasing all proof of the existence of those who had been condemned to death. She inspired her friends, helping them fight off depression with her encouragement. She was a shining spark, lighting the darkness of our miserable existence.

My greatest sources of inspiration were the girls from Hungary. In general, the Hungarian girls were much stronger than the girls from Poland. Unlike us, they had not undergone years of hunger and suffering in a ghetto before being transported to Auschwitz. Their inner reserves of strength had not been sapped over the long months of pain. They had not been forced to watch as parents and siblings died of disease, hunger and Nazi bullets. Hungary had been left alone until 1944, and the Hungarian girls in Auschwitz were much more audacious and daring in their attempts to preserve their *frumkeit*.

It was *Yom Kippur*, and most of the Polish girls refused to fast. "Why should I fast?" was the general opinion. "I fast the entire year anyway." The Hungarian girls, however, were much more stubborn. They were standing outside the block, offering their meager bowls of soup to anyone who wasn't fasting themselves. I remember standing next to one Hungarian girl, devouring her bowl of soup with hungry eyes. Then I turned away. I wasn't going to eat on *Yom Kippur*, but I didn't have the strength of these Hungarian girls. How could they be so courageous? I wasn't eating, but I couldn't bear to stand there, smiling, offering my food to someone else. I envied their strength and fortitude.

There was one Hungarian girl who came to Auschwitz in late spring of 1944. By some miracle, the *chassidishe* girl had managed to smuggle in a small *siddur* she had been given by her father. The little *siddur* became the greatest treasure and the biggest secret in our entire block.

Not only did the *siddur* have all the *tefillos,* it also contained the entire *Sefer Tehillim* and had a Jewish calendar pasted into the inside cover. With that little *siddur* we were able to determine when it was *Rosh Chodesh* and when it was *Yom Tov.* We used to wait until the *blokowa* went off for a drink before we all gathered around the girl to listen to her say some *Tehillim.* She used to read to us in a quiet, clear voice, emphasizing the meaning of every *passuk.* Most of the time, we didn't get a chance to pull out the little *siddur* until late at night. Then the girl's voice rang softly through the darkness, and we all stared, mesmerized, at the small ray of light that shone through the narrow window to rest directly on the page from which she was reading.

In those few moments, we were all able to temporarily forget our miserable surroundings and lift ourselves up out of our sordid reality. We all knew that if we were caught, we would be put to death without hesitation. But even the thought of the gas chambers couldn't stop us from snatching those few moments to lift our spirits out of the gutter.

Although I was no longer in Auschwitz the following *Pesach,* I did hear reports about it later. As the *Yom Tov* approached, the mood in the camp was bitter and depressed. One girl kept repeating in a singsong, *"Avadim hayinu l'Hitler b'Auschwitz."* No one gave any thought to the *Yom Tov* itself. But the girl with the *siddur* had other ideas.

"Come to my *pritch* on *seder* night," she urged all of us. "We'll have a *seder,* you'll see."

Most of them thought that she had finally snapped.

Where was she going to get a *seder* from in Auschwitz? She had no *matzoh*, no *marror*, no wine. Still, most of them were curious enough to assemble at her *pritch* on the first night of *Pesach* to see what would happen.

The girl sat cross-legged on her *pritch*, eyes glowing.

"Imagine," she said softly. "Imagine that you are lighting the candles for *Yom Tov*. See, they are shining so brightly! Now we are sitting down at the *seder*. Close your eyes! Can't you taste the sweet wine of the first cup on your tongue? Now we are washing our hands for *karpas* . . ."

She held everyone spellbound as she read the *Haggadah* from her little *siddur*. They all found themselves dipping their fingers into non-existent cups of wine, spilling out ten drops as she quietly recited the Ten Plagues. They all said *"Amen!"* as she read the final *brachah* of *Maggid*, and they all joined in as she sang *Hallel*. Tears streamed down everyone's cheeks as they finished the imitation *seder*. The emotions they experienced were too roiled and complex to fit into the molds of description. What were they really feeling? Joy? Misery? Depression? They themselves did not know.

There were girls who worked in the "Kanada" commando, sorting and classifying the myriad items stolen from the Jews. Once, they came across candles. Those girls risked their lives by stealing the candles. If they had been caught smuggling anything out, they would have been killed instantly. Fortunately, they managed to get the candles out of the commando in safety.

They brought their prize triumphantly back to the block. Girls gathered around, exclaiming excitedly. And that *Shabbos*, several girls were able to fulfill the *mitzvah* of lighting candles. A hush fell over the block as heads bowed over the candles, whispering the *brachah* with painful devotion.

Again, it was mostly the Hungarian girls who lit the candles, but many of the Polish women did as well. One particular woman, Mrs. Ryvka Weiser, often traded her bread for candles on *Erev Shabbos*. As a married woman, it was a *mitzvah* for her to light, and she was determined not to miss a single week. She told me years later that she felt certain that she and her daughter had survived Auschwitz in the *zchus* of her *Shabbos* candles. I watched with awe and delight, but I was unaccustomed to the idea of single girls lighting candles for *Shabbos*, so I didn't light myself. I just watched, feasting my eyes on the lovely sight of *Shabbos* candles. Those of us who were not lighting covered for the girls who did, often sitting innocently on the ground right in front of the candles to hide them from the prying eyes of our *kapos*.

Aviezer Burstyn was a young man who was forced to work in the "sewage commando." He had to collect human waste from the latrines all over the camp. The only advantage was that it gave him the opportunity to act as a liaison between the men's and women's camp. He also had access to the block where all the plunder taken from the Jews was kept, and he often managed to smuggle things out to help alleviate the suffering of his fellow victims.

Many of the women approached him and asked him to get them warm clothing. Happy to be of assistance, he smuggled sweaters, socks, shoes and warm clothing to the women's camp in his pail. Most of the girls, however, could not bring themselves to speak directly to a young man. Many of them asked the older women to act as intermediaries for them, asking Aviezer for the things they so desperately needed.

One day, Aviezer was surprised to see a young girl approaching him. She came forward hesitantly, looking as if she would turn and flee at the slightest provocation. Aviezer gently asked her if he could be of any help.

At first, she didn't answer. She was about fifteen, and skinny as a skeleton. An entire world of suffering seemed to be expressed in her face. When Aviezer repeated his question, she answered him in a voice so low he could barely make out what she was saying. He nodded and smiled, promising to get her what she had asked for as soon as possible.

The very next day, Aviezer managed to "organize" a sweater for the girl. He stuffed it into his pail and managed to get across to the women's camp without raising any alarm. He saw the girl waiting for him anxiously, and he pulled the sweater out of his pail and handed it to her, waiting to see her face light up.

Instead, tears spilled out of her huge, dark eyes and slid silently down her cheeks as she slowly took the sweater. Aviezer was appalled.

"What happened?" he asked urgently. "I brought you a sweater of the finest wool. Don't you like it?"

"I didn't ask for a sweater," she whispered in a trembling voice. "I asked for a *siddur*, so I can *daven*."

Aviezer realized that he had misunderstood her whispered answer. She didn't want a sweater to warm her body; she wanted a *siddur* to warm her soul.

Sarah and I were dismayed to discover that our Aunt Bluma was also in Auschwitz. Her story was a sad and depressing one. After her sister died, she married David, her sister's husband, and became a mother to his six children. Poor Aunt Bluma had to watch as her husband and three of

159

her stepchildren died from disease and hunger in the ghetto. The two beautiful little girls that she had given birth to were taken in the *shpero*. She had already suffered so much, and now she was going through the agonies of Auschwitz!

She was living in Block Twenty, right next to us. Whenever we were spared the torments of the *appell*, we used to go and speak to her. As terrible as it was that she had to be there, we were grateful to have a member of the family nearby.

Two of her stepdaughters, Perele and Kayla, were also with her. Out of eight children, Perele and Kayla were the only ones who survived. Sarah and I spent many hours together with our cousins, wistfully recalling happier times when life had actually been normal and carefree.

I'll never forget the time when I saw Kayla risk her life to get a little soup. We were all standing in line outside our blocks to receive our meager portions of soup. The *kapos* and *blokowas* were walking up and down the line, slapping their truncheons against their palms for emphasis. Vicious dogs strained against their leashes, eager to pounce on a helpless Jew when given the command. Suddenly, I saw Kayla darting up the road toward the kettles of soup. It took her only a second or two to dip a small pot into one of the kettles and hurry back into line. I stared at her, open-mouthed. How did she do that? How could she risk it? How did she manage to get away with it without getting caught?

I watched as she quickly ran back into Block Twenty with the precious pot of stolen soup. Curious, I followed her into the block to find out what had prompted her to risk her life. There, sitting on a *pritch*, was Aunt Bluma, slowly drinking soup out of the little pot.

"Kayla!" I said with a little gasp. "I-I don't believe it! What made you do that? Why did you—"

It was Aunt Bluma who replied. "Kayla has arranged food for me before," she said. "What bothers me the most is that after all that, you would think she would at least taste a little bit of the soup that she gets for me. But she makes me drink every last drop."

Somehow, I wasn't surprised. Kayla endangered her life so that her mother could have a little more soup. I was proud of my cousin, and I was happy that she was there to make Aunt Bluma's plight a little easier.

*Baruch Hashem,* the three of them survived the war. They were transferred to a labor camp shortly after this incident, and they were liberated by the Allied forces in 1945.

# CHAPTER 20

---■---

# Tefillos and Tefillin

WONDERFUL STORIES DRIFTED THROUGH THE FENCES from the men's camp, stories of warmth and inspiration that gave me the courage to keep going. It was comforting to know that the men were waging the same silent war against the Nazis. They, too, insisted on remaining *betzelem Elokim* and refused to degenerate into bestial animals without any vestige of humanity.

Zalman Gradowski, Milton Buki, Rabbi Leib Langfuss, Zalman Loewenthal—these names as well as others were on the list of *Sondercommandos* who stubbornly got together each day to form a *minyan* to *daven*. They refused to allow their surroundings to turn them away from their faith in the *Ribono Shel Olam*. Day after day, they risked discovery and death to gather together to pray.

The irreligious inmates watched in disbelief. Surrounded
by murder and brutality, how could they raise their voices in
praise of Hashem's mercy? They were forced to witness the
gassing of their relatives; why didn't they succumb to bitter-
ness and turn away from *Yiddishkeit*? How could they glorify
Hashem's name when His people were being slaughtered just
for being Jews? Try as they might, they could not understand
the depth of *emunah* that their religious friends possessed;
they couldn't comprehend their steadfast belief that all this
was part of Hashem's plan.

There were a few, however, who found themselves up-
lifted by the beauty of the moment. The soft, haunting
melody of *Lecha Dodi* was often enough to bring a person to
tears. Who knows what memories were brought to life within
the minds of the embittered victims of Auschwitz? Perhaps a
voice whispered, "Do you remember the *shul* on Friday night,
sparkling with the lights of dozens of candles? Can you
picture the swaying bodies as the men earnestly whispered
their prayers? How can you ever forget sitting at the *Shabbos*
table, surrounded by a loving family?" And then, falteringly,
another man would step forward to join the little *minyan*. Yet
another *neshamah* had been inspired to quietly defy the death
machines of Auschwitz.

Years later, my husband would often tell me how he and
his friends would sneak out of their barracks before *appell* to
put on *tefillin*. There was a young man who had managed to
smuggle his *tefillin* into the camp, and dozens of men and
boys lined up every morning for the priceless opportunity to
wear *tefillin*, if only for a few seconds. The boy guarded his
*tefillin* as if they were made of solid gold, but he generously
allowed anyone to wear them.

Each person hurriedly wound the *retzuah* around his arm.

There was little time to savor the exquisite joy of performing the *mitzvah* of wearing *tefillin;* not only was there the constant fear of discovery, which would have resulted in a severe beating at best and a quick trip to the crematorium at worst, but there were dozens and dozens of men waiting impatiently for the chance to put *tefillin* on themselves. A heartfelt *brachah* whispered under his breath was all each person had time for; then he would quickly remove the *tefillin* and hand the precious *mitzvah* on to the next person in line.

We also heard that a man from Hungary had managed to smuggle his *tallis* and *tefillin* into the Buna branch of Auschwitz. When the inmates were lined up for *appell,* waiting for a German to come and count them, the *tefillin* would pass from hand to hand, each man getting a few precious moments to wear them before passing them on to the next man in line. One person would stand guard, keeping an eye out for the approach of a Nazi. The moment a uniform was sighted in the distance, a hissed signal would cause the *tefillin* to promptly disappear. By the time the Nazi arrived on the scene, all he saw were lines of silent men, waiting with expressionless faces to be counted by their tormentors. There was nothing to indicate that a profound revolution against the Nazi terror had just taken place.

Men risked their lives day after day for the chance to do a single *mitzvah.* The most audacious schemes were carried out, often with a large amount of success. It wasn't only the *frum* people, however; even those that had been non-religious joined the lines of men waiting for a chance to wear *tefillin.* A *mitzvah* was something tangible to cling to in the midst of all the horrors and despair.

There was a young man named Hershel Protzel who broke his foot in the coal mines. His friends, frantic in their efforts to save him from the selections, tried hiding him in the barracks and covering for him at work, fulfilling his quota as well as their own. When they saw that he was not getting any better, they managed to pull enough strings to get him a job as latrine commando. His task was to keep the lines of people waiting for the latrine in order by issuing numbers and keeping track. He was able to do his job and stay off his broken foot without any difficulty.

Hershel took advantage of the situation. He managed to get a pair of *tefillin*. He hid the smuggled treasure in a hole in the roof of a shed, right next to the latrines. Suddenly, Hershel's latrine became the most popular one in that section of Auschwitz. Men waited impatiently in line for the chance to savor a moment of *tefillah* while wearing *tefillin*.

Hershel, who managed to survive the death marches on his broken foot, always maintained that it was the *zchus* of *tefillin* that kept him alive.

# CHAPTER 21

∎

# A Journey to the Left

VERYONE WHO ENTERED THE GATES OF AUSCHWITZ expected to die in one way or another. Perhaps it would be the gas chambers; maybe it would be a bullet in the heart. There were so many ways to die, and no way to live.

Somehow, though, those who weren't immediately gassed to death clung to the hope that maybe, just maybe, there would be a way to survive. Perhaps the war would end before they were selected for death; maybe the Russians would take over Auschwitz and release all the prisoners. Most people clung to their daydreams of rescue. I, too, dreamed of a miraculous escape; I thought that I might be able to find a way out of Auschwitz through the sewer pipes. I held as tightly as I could to hope, because that was all I had.

The problem was that the glimpses of hope were so faint. There were times when the agony grew so intense that many women lost their minds and electrocuted themselves on the fences, finding it easier to die than to continue suffering. *Baruch Hashem,* I had Sarah with me to keep me sane, but one incident remains so vivid that it still haunts me, decades later.

Block Thirty-One was being punished. We were locked into our barracks for three days with nothing to eat. I was lying on my *pritch* together with four other girls. None of us had the energy to move around. We were apathetic and lethargic, waiting dully for something to happen.

On the third day, we were given food. The sadistic Nazis rubbed salt in our wounds; we were given soup to eat in a huge fifteen-quart pot with no spoon and no way to eat it. I remember the five of us sitting there, staring at the pot. The sickly-looking liquid barely covered the bottom of the huge container. Finally, I picked up the pot and tipped it forward, trying to drink straight from the large vessel.

It was as if something had snapped. One of the girls grabbed the pot from my hands and threw herself backwards, tilting the pot up so that the soup would pour into her mouth. The other three girls also pounced on the pot, scooping up the soup with their hands.

I felt sick as I watched them. They looked like a pack of mangy dogs fighting over an old bone. I started crying, more from humiliation than hunger. I couldn't believe the depths we had reached in our desperation.

The others stopped their frantic gobbling to look at me. Glancing sheepishly at each other, they handed the pot back to me, offering me the rest of the soup. I couldn't bring myself to use my hands to eat it; I felt an overwhelming wave of nausea and a choking sensation back in my throat. The girls, their hunger completely forgotten, gently helped me hold the pot. They told me to cup my hands together, and they poured the leftover soup into my cupped hands. I slowly sipped the liquid, grimacing at the taste; still, it was food, and I finished the rest of the soup. As I drank from my palms, one of the girls cupped her hands underneath mine so she could catch any spilled drops, while another licked a few droplets from her filthy blanket.

I couldn't stop crying. How could we sink so low? How could we turn into animals like this? I felt a wave of incredible hatred for the Germans for doing this to us. They were turning us into beasts, taking away any last scraps of dignity. I crawled off the *pritch* and went looking for Sarah. She was the only reason I had for resisting death.

It was late 1944 when Dr. Mengele decided that Sarah was no longer worth keeping alive.

We were standing at *appell,* slowly passing by Mengele. His terrifying thumb pronounced life and death sentences. To the right—life. To the left—death. Each girl was casually looked over before being judged. We never knew what whim would strike him, and whether we would be alive at the end of the day.

As Sarah approached him, his thumb pointed toward the left. As she stumbled into the line of death, I didn't even look at Mengele to see which way he was pointing for me. I just followed Sarah to the left.

The left line was led away. We were two of five thousand girls selected for the gas chambers. We were stuffed into a narrow barracks and left waiting for the end. We didn't get any food, and we couldn't even sit down because there wasn't enough room. We stood there trembling for hours, awaiting the moment of death.

The *appell* had taken place in the early morning, but we were not taken out of the barracks until dusk. It slowly grew dark as the column of five thousand girls were led to the gas chambers.

Bemused, I thought of the *Marranos* in Spain, the *kedoshim* that died in 1648-49 in Poland and the countless martyrs throughout the ages who had preferred death to conversion. The universal cry of *"Shema Yisrael"* echoed in my mind. This is what we had become, was it not? Martyrs, Jews dying for no other reason than their Jewishness.

None of us spoke. Nobody cried or pleaded for mercy. It was as if we had all made a pact to retain our dignity and deny the Nazis the satisfaction of watching us grovel.

Our line came to a halt. The crowd was too thick for me to see what was happening in front. After a while, I saw heavy smoke braided with glistening sparks rising to the sky. The smoke hung in the air for several moments before dissipating.

I clung tightly to Sarah's hand. When I glanced at her, her eyes were huge and round, staring in silence at the thick, ugly smoke. Neither of us said a word. I was almost impatient to get into the gas chamber and get my life over with. Soon it would be over, all over, and we would be at peace.

By this time, we were close enough to the front of the line to see what was happening. There was a large building ahead of us with steel doors. The doors opened, and a group of people were forced into the chamber. When the chamber was packed full, the doors were sealed shut. SS men with dogs and machine guns guarded the line, walking up and down the column to ensure that nobody tried to escape. At each cut-off point, when the chamber was full and there was no more room for the next girl to enter, the Nazis would draw a truncheon across the line of the first five girls in the column who were waiting their turn to enter the gates of death. Then, when the last vestiges of smoke had spiraled upwards and faded out of existence, the truncheon would lift up and the next group of girls would be herded into the gas chamber.

I slowly moved forward, almost an automaton. Sarah and I drew closer and closer to the front of the line. The column was slowly melting, girls vanishing into the chamber and dissolving into ashes.

Suddenly, I felt the truncheon on my chest. Directly in front of me, the steel doors ponderously closed. We were next. I touched Sarah's hand again, making sure that she was standing next to me. Soon, I promised her silently. Soon, very soon, it will all be over.

Then the eerie silence was broken by shouts and curses. My mind froze, and I stood there stupidly.

"*Umdrehen! Mach los! Schnell du Schwein!* Turn around! Go! Run fast, you swine!" The Nazis were shouting at us, but I was too confused to understand what they were saying. A blow on the head shocked me out of my numbness, and Sarah was pulling on my arm. She turned me around and gave me a shove in the right direction. We were running along with the rest of the girls in the column, away from the gas chambers, urged on by shouts and whips. I had no idea what was going on. My mind seemed to be smothered in a fog of bewilderment. I just stumbled after Sarah mechanically.

We were roughly herded into a building and ordered to bathe and be disinfected. I was shaken to the core, and all I could think of was that they were trying to trick us; it must be some kind of sadistic Nazi joke, making us think that we were going to live and then dashing our hopes in the gas chambers.

Evidently, I wasn't the only person who thought this, because a piercing cry suddenly rang out. Someone was screaming in terror, cowering in the back of the stuffy bathhouse. The cry was taken up by others, and the bathhouse rang with our screams and shrieks. I found myself screaming along with the rest of the girls. I couldn't seem to help myself. All the terror, all the horrors we had witnessed seemed to culminate in that little room and drain all our sanity. We were in a collective panic, drowning in an ocean of screams and dread.

The girls working in the bathhouse tried to calm us down. "It's true, it's true," one of them said. "You have really escaped death. An order came in from Germany, requesting five hundred slaves. Better slaves than ashes," she whispered with tears in her eyes. "You still have a spark of hope."

The girl turned away. After a moment, she continued, her voice muffled. "The Nazis want no witnesses. I would gladly trade places with you. You, at least, have a chance of survival. We will all be sent to the gas chambers in a few weeks. Everyone who works in the bathhouses is slated for death. Oh, I would gladly trade places with you! Better slaves than ashes . . ." Her voice broke, and she began to sob.

The bathhouse was silent. The panic seemed to drain away, leaving us mute. We entered the bathing rooms without a word.

After the bath and disinfection, we were each given a dress and a pair of wooden shoes. Some girls were lucky, and got leather shoes instead of wooden clogs. Sarah was one of the lucky ones.

We were marched outside to find several trucks waiting for us. We clambered aboard the trucks, once again squeezed tightly together. The trucks shifted into gear and lumbered off into the night. We were being taken out of Auschwitz to become slaves somewhere in Germany.

As we swayed back and forth in the truck, I conjured up the image of my father in my mind. I could picture him talking to me, giving me calm words of encouragement. I remembered how he used to quote the Talmud: "Do not lose hope, even when the sword is at your throat." I promised him silently that I, too, would not lose faith in Hashem. I would make sure Sarah and I survived the war.

# CHAPTER 22

—————————————■—————————————

# A Moment of Weakness

THE NIGHT SLOWLY GAVE WAY TO DAWN AS OUR journey dragged itself on and on. Several hours into the morning, we reached a town. The truck stopped for a few moments, and I managed to peek through a crack in the wall and look outside.

I was astounded to see a world that I had almost forgotten about. Sunlight still existed? Children still played on green grass? There were manicured lawns, tall trees and stately houses. Several feet away from the truck, a little girl scampered after some butterflies, giggling with delight. I stared with disbelief at the pink dress she wore, with the white ruffled petticoats showing underneath.

The truck lurched forward, and I lost sight of the little girl, but I couldn't get the picture out of my head. What had our

Jewish children done that they deserved to be cut off from such an existence? How could there still be laughter in a world tainted by the smoke of Auschwitz?

I found no answer. All I could do was go on.

Night had fallen once again before the truck finally groaned to a halt. The back doors crashed open, and we were ordered off the trucks and arranged into columns. With the usual kicks and shouts, we began to march.

Two weary hours later, we reached a forest. Five dilapidated vans were waiting there, their engines idling. We were herded into the vans and driven off. Once again our world had shrunk to one of lurching movement and dreary darkness. We didn't know where we were going; all we knew was that we would be slaves when we got there. Better slaves than ashes, I reminded myself. I clung desperately to that thought.

The only thing that kept me going at that point was the thought of Sarah. I turned to speak to her, but she was gone! I stared at the strange girl standing next to me with shock. What had happened to Sarah? Where was she? I tried to shout her name, but it came out as a hoarse croak. I felt overwhelmingly dizzy. There seemed to be a commotion a few feet away; girls were being shoved aside. I tried to see what was happening, but the terror I felt at Sarah's disappearance seemed to be affecting my eyesight, and I couldn't see properly. The last thing I saw was Sarah pushing her way towards me. Then my vision darkened completely, and I fainted.

I don't know how long it took me to regain consciousness, but the first thing I was aware of was the touch of Sarah's hand. She was supporting my weight, trying to keep me from falling. I realized dully that the sensation of movement had stopped. Sarah and another girl were trying to get me out of the van.

I had no idea what was going on. I mumbled something, begging them to leave me alone and let me go to sleep, but Sarah persisted. She dragged me bodily out of the van and propped me up on my feet. Once again, we were ordered to march. I followed Sarah's lead mechanically without actually being aware of what I was doing. She seemed to be speaking to me, but her voice sounded like it was coming from hundreds of miles away.

We marched through what was left of the night. The sky was beginning to pale in the east before we finally reached the Schrohl spinning factory. We filed slowly into the empty, gray structure, the building that was to be our workplace as long as we survived the concentration camp.

The gigantic room lay veiled in shadow. As we all came to a halt, a frightful stillness seemed to settle over us like a smothering blanket. For several heartbeats, the stillness lingered; then a sudden hissing broke the silence. We all jumped, startled by the noise.

The hissing sounded again, and I realized that it was coming from the ceiling. I craned my neck and saw huge pipes crisscrossing the room. As I stared at them, I felt a choking sensation. The pipes were moving! They were moving downwards, coming down to crush us, to bury us underneath them . . . The room was spinning. I tried to shout a warning, but I couldn't make a sound. Didn't anyone see? Couldn't anyone stop it?

There was a timeless stretch of darkness before water splashed against my face. Sarah's voice echoed in my ears. "Please, Chanka, not here! Not now! Don't leave me alone." And then, somewhat louder, I heard her voice again. "She'll be all right. She's just tired, that's all. She's a very hard worker, and we've both worked with spinning machines before! We'll both be very useful, you'll see!"

Sarah, I thought drowsily, you know that Tatteshe said we should never lie. We've never stepped foot in a factory before in our lives. Maybe they thought that since we were from Lodz, with all its industrial factories, we would have some experience. But really, Sarah, you shouldn't tell lies like that. Who are you talking to anyway?

I opened my eyes. Why was I lying on the ground? As I struggled to sit up, two girls helped me to my feet and gently propped me against a wall. Sarah, smiling through her tears, was gently sponging my face with a wet cloth.

I don't know why I collapsed at Schrohl when I had managed to survive the gas chambers at Auschwitz. I found out later that the SS women had wanted to shoot me, but Sarah convinced them that I was a good, steady worker and would be much more useful if I was left alive. They allowed her to wipe my face with a wet cloth, and the soothing coolness was enough to bring me back to my senses, thus saving my life. As the girls joked afterwards, I was the only one to be initiated into Schrohl with water after all the filth and dirt of Auschwitz.

# CHAPTER 23

■

## Slave Trade

R. SCHROHL'S TEXTILE FACTORY WAS JUST OUTSIDE
the town of Halbstadt. He needed fifty textile
experts for his factory, and the government told
him he could have his experts if he agreed to house and feed
five hundred slaves for the ammunition factory nearby.
When the contingent of slaves arrived at the ammunition
factory from Auschwitz, fifty girls were chosen to be textile
specialists and sent on to the textile factory. Sarah's daring
enabled the two of us to be among the lucky ones. It was
considered very fortunate, because we weren't working in a
factory that would be a target of the Allies.

On the first day of my slave labor, I was assigned to a huge
spinning machine. I stared at the contraption with bewilderment. I was supposed to work this thing? I had never seen

anything like it in my life! I understood that the machine was supposed to spin cotton into thread, but how I was supposed to make the machine do its job was completely beyond my comprehension.

I almost panicked when an SS guard strode up to my machine, with a middle-aged German woman in tow. The woman began to speak in rapid German, instructing me in how to use the machine. Nervously trying to ignore the guard looming over me with his rifle, I concentrated on my instructions. I knew that my continued survival depended on my ability to make myself useful.

With shaking hands, I took the hot spool and obeyed the woman's instructions. I attached a thread to the spool, fed it through several holes and connected it to the soft, dangling cotton cord. I held my breath as I started up the machine. For one agonizing moment, nothing happened; then the machine's gears rumbled into action, and I breathed a sigh of relief when I saw that it was spinning smoothly. So far, so good. I was thoroughly drenched with sweat, but at least I was still alive.

The guard watched me for a few moments, patting his rifle absently. Then he turned away and led the German woman to another machine to give her some further instructions.

I spent the entire day in a state of anxiety. The machines were old and often got clogged. Each of us wore a white apron to collect all the bits of cotton waste, which were put together in a large barrel to be spun again. I had to watch very carefully, making sure that the spools continued spinning evenly and no cotton waste got caught in the gears.

I glanced often in Sarah's direction, but she seemed to be doing fine. She smiled at me, but neither of us said a word;

we had already been warned that any talking was strictly forbidden. The hours dragged slowly by, accentuated by the idea that we had been given almost nothing to eat since our arrival.

I had long since come to terms with the fact that there was no way Sarah and I could survive the war without help. The little we were given by the Germans was not enough to keep body and soul together. If we did not get assistance from some other source, there was no question in my mind that we would starve to death. But where could we turn for help? The Nazis? The SS officers? Were there any decent human beings left in the world, any person who would treat a Jew with grace and dignity?

Sarah and I had our share of miracles and pain-ridden obstacles. The little stubble of hair that was slowly growing back didn't help our appearance, but somehow it made Sarah look like an endearing little boy. More than once, a German took pity on the "lad" and provided "him" with an extra bit of bread. These little windfalls, which Sarah always shared with me, were a tremendous help to us.

However, we were not the only ones in such a desperate situation; every other girl in the labor camp was in the same dire straits. Again and again, I would watch with resignation as someone would spot Sarah's benefactor and beg for a piece of bread. The news that someone was nearby with food would spread like wildfire, and crowds of girls would converge around the German, pleading for something to eat. The usual result was that the German, frightened by all the attention, would hurry away, leaving us without our benefactor. I couldn't blame the other girls; they were as hungry as we were. But I couldn't help wishing guiltily that nobody would notice when someone gave Sarah a piece of bread, so that the two of us could have some food of our own to eat in peace.

Late one afternoon, as I was standing over my spinning machine, I was frightened out of my wits by the sudden appearance of a tall, broad-shouldered peasant woman. She stood towering over me, hands on her hips and a scowl twisting her mouth. I shuddered as I saw that her left eye was sewn shut. I felt my own eyes widen with terror as she leaned forward, peering into my face. What did she want from me? I cast a quick glance over toward the SS woman. She was sitting on a chair, chewing on a fat sandwich; she seemed oblivious to what was going on. The peasant woman standing in front of me followed my gaze and scowled again. Oh, Hashem, what does she want? Why did she pick me? What should I do?

Slowly, I tried to back away from her, but she swiftly moved forward, blocking my way. Looking toward the guard again, she drew a finger across her throat and snarled, *"Ich und du kaput!* You and I are finished!"

My mouth went dry. Was she some kind of spy? She was saying something else, but I couldn't understand a word. She kept repeating the same strange phrase over and over again, *"Ohlle, die Luder!"* I had no idea what it meant, but it sounded very nasty.

Yet maybe she was indeed a friend. Whenever she repeated that phrase, she made a nasty face at the guards. But if she was an enemy of the Nazis, what was she doing in the textile plant? Was she one of the workers? She was wearing a white apron just like the rest of us. If she *was* a friend, what would happen to me if I was caught talking to her? If she wasn't supposed to be there, there was a very strong chance that I would be sent back to perish in Auschwitz, or merely shot down on the spot.

I looked at the SS woman again. She was still busy enjoying her lunch, spicing it with the sadistic knowledge that she was eating a hearty meal in front of the starving eyes of fifty hungry girls. She hadn't noticed the peasant woman at all. I glanced back at the peasant woman, who nodded at me. Then the peasant woman pointed at her apron and headed towards the door.

I was completely bewildered. Why had she troubled to go through the whole rigmarole if she was just going to leave without doing anything? Maybe she was just trying to frighten me.

As the woman neared the entrance, she swerved to the right so she could empty the cotton waste out of her apron. She gave me one last significant look before vanishing through the door.

I tried to relax. The strange peasant woman was gone, and none of the guards had interfered. The whole episode was over.

The problem was that I didn't understand what had happened. Somehow, I found myself wanting to trust that strange, ugly, one-eyed woman. I wished I knew what she was trying to tell me.

I snapped out of my reverie when one of the spools at the front of my machine started to get snarled up. I delicately untangled the knots, my mind elsewhere. Just as I finished putting the spool back into place, a movement made me look up.

I was standing directly in front of a tiny, grimy window, the only one in the entire building. The peasant woman was standing outside the window, gesturing to me. She began sidling over, edging out of my view.

Instinctively, I moved in the same direction. Her face lit up with a grin, and she nodded vigorously at me. She waved at me with one hand, motioning that I should keep moving to the right.

As I moved slowly away from my spinning machine, I couldn't believe that I was actually taking the risk of being caught. I could get punished for neglecting my job. Besides, the whole thing might be a trap. Somehow, though, I was convinced that I had to find out what the strange peasant woman was doing.

I realized that I was heading directly toward the waste bin where the woman had emptied her apron. Holding my head a little higher, I walked toward the bin, relieved to have a decent excuse for being away from my post. My apron was nearly full, anyway, so I could say that I was emptying the cotton waste out of my apron so I could continue working.

I walked up to the crate and started shaking out my apron. The crate was three-quarters full of cotton waste, but there was a small V-shaped piece of paper tucked into the corner. I was surprised to see the paper; after all, the only thing that was ever put in the crate was cotton waste, and paper was a very precious commodity!

Puzzled, I slowly reached for the inch-long piece of paper. When I moved some of the cotton waste aside, I discovered that the piece of paper was actually a white paper package, soft to the touch. A soft package. Maybe—just maybe—it was food!

Without turning my head, I glanced toward the chair where the SS woman had been sitting. The chair was empty! I started to shake. Where was she? She could be anywhere, looking at anyone—including me! Maybe she was standing right behind me!

I told myself sternly to stop panicking. If it was a trap, it was already sprung, and I was doomed. Besides, the thought of food was so overwhelmingly tempting that I couldn't resist. My hand darted into the bin, grabbed the package and slipped it into my apron. Then, with my heart pounding twice as fast as usual, I slowly turned around and headed back to my spinning machine.

*Baruch Hashem!* I almost collapsed with relief when I saw that the SS woman was on the other side of the room, completely ignoring me. So far, so good. The peasant woman was not trying to trap me, and now I had the package she had risked her life to give me. It was so soft that it had to be a piece of bread. Just the thought of a piece of bread had my mouth watering, but I knew that I still had a problem. The guard often checked the contents of our aprons. I had to get rid of the package, but I wanted to share it with Sarah, too. I racked my brains for a way to open the package in safety together with my sister.

I was too preoccupied with the precious contents of my apron to pay any particular attention to my machine, and the spools kept clogging. Sarah, who was working on a machine close by, was alarmed at my apparent lack of concentration. She anxiously hurried over to give me a hand, and I took advantage of the opportunity to let her know what was going on.

As she leaned over to help untangle one of the spools, I took her right hand and put it in my apron. Her eyes widened as she felt the soft package nestled among the bits of cotton. I mouthed the word "toilet," and she nodded her understanding. Without looking at each other, we finished repairing the machine. Sarah went back to her own machine, but I could tell she was watching me closely.

183

I waited several minutes before asking the SS guard for permission to go to the toilet. When she nodded at me, I hurried into the small, fetid room and waited impatiently for Sarah to come. It seemed like hours before she finally arrived. As soon as my sister came into the room, I pulled the package out of my apron with shaking hands and eagerly ripped it open.

Sarah and I stared in disbelief. There were two slices of fresh bread lying in my hands. Bread! There was one piece of white bread and one of black, with a thick slab of white cheese. I almost cried over that sandwich. I had never seen anything more beautiful in my life.

I quickly divided the sandwich in two and gave half of it to Sarah. We quickly devoured the cheese and bread, marvelling over the taste of food that wasn't spoiled or moldy. I threw the white paper deep into the latrine, and the two of us returned to our posts as nonchalantly as possible, pretending nothing had happened.

I worked mechanically for the remainder of the day. I couldn't get the picture of that peasant woman out of my mind. What had prompted her to act so mercifully? What made a German woman risk her life to give a little food to a Jewish slave girl? Could it be that common human decency really still existed?

For seven full months, that peasant woman never failed to miss a single day. Every afternoon, when the SS woman wasn't looking, I would make my way to the waste bin and dig out the small, life-giving package hidden among the cotton balls. It was usually bread and cheese; sometimes, on Sundays, the bread was filled with some kind of blueberry preserve. I am convinced that Sarah and I would have either starved to death or succumbed to some kind of disease if not for the nourishing food that the woman provided us with every single day. That small act of human kindness was the only comfort the two of us had during that horrible, miserable year in the slave camp of Halbstadt.

# BOOK FOUR

---■---

# The
# Ravages
# of the
# Storm

# CHAPTER 24

————————■————————

# The End of Winter

THE CONCENTRATION CAMP WHERE WE WERE HOUSED was a slave labor camp, and conditions were miserable. We were given next to nothing to eat, and the water ration was barely enough to prevent dehydration. Our barracks had no heat, even in the winter, and the buildings were infested with lice and bugs. Still, we had much to be thankful for. There were no gas chambers, no crematoriums and no forced marches.

In the early months of 1945, we were forced to witness the systematic bloodshed taking place on the lonely, winding roads. Through a grimy window in our barracks, I was able to see the long, winding columns of Jews being marched to their deaths. Day and night, in the heart of winter, the death marches plodded past our camp. There was no rhyme or

189

reason to the marches; their purpose was simply to wear the victims down to their deaths. Some of the people were wrapped in tattered blankets, but most of the Jews had only rags to keep out the biting wind. They had nothing to eat and drink, and they were never allowed to rest. I watched with tears streaming down my cheeks as men and women falteringly bent down to scoop up a little snow to eat. Anyone who stumbled never got up again; a few bullets made sure of that. There was nothing I could do but watch helplessly as thousands of my fellow Jews died.

The Nazis had remarked often enough that they would make sure we all died before they themselves surrendered. They knew their barbarity would only augment their punishment, and they wanted to hide the cruelty of the concentration camps from the liberating forces. The simplest way to conceal the death camps was to make sure that the inmates were all dead. Much as we rejoiced to find out that the war was going badly for the Germans, it was frightening to know that we had a very slim chance of surviving long enough to be liberated.

One night, as Sarah and I returned to the concentration camp from the textile factory, I felt a strange undercurrent of anxiety in the camp. I could almost touch the sensations of fear and anticipation. Something was happening, something unexpected. I wondered uneasily if we would find ourselves yanked off our *pritches* and sent marching off into the night, with no destination except death. Would we join the thousands of innocent victims who were forced to walk and walk and walk until they collapsed lifeless in the snow?

As I entered the barracks, the tension was so thick I could have cut it with a knife. The girls were huddled on their *pritches*, unnaturally silent. One girl pulled me over, signalling that I should keep quiet.

"Behave normally," she whispered. "Don't say a word. Go to your bunk and cover your head with your blanket. Pretend that you're asleep. We've found out that the entire camp is mined, and we're surrounded by sub-machine guns. Any sign of excitement might provoke the Germans into killing us all."

I was flooded with conflicting emotions. I felt incredible joy; we all knew that the marches were a sign of German defeat, and the mining of the camp meant that the Nazis expected to be occupied by the Allies or the Russians momentarily. I felt absolute terror; surely we all wouldn't die now, only hours before liberation! It couldn't be!

I lay down on my *pritch*, but sleep was impossible. I listened to the uneven breathing of my fellow inmates and knew that no one else was sleeping, either. We spent the night in a fearful state of anticipation and apprehension. Anyone glancing into our barracks would have seen us all apparently sound asleep, but not a single girl actually got any sleep that entire night. We were all too uneasy about the future to even think about sleeping.

The camp was unusually noisy that night. Once, when I peeked out from underneath my blanket, I saw SS women scurrying back and forth, packing and carrying packages and loading them onto trucks. The head SS guard was giving orders to her subordinates in a hushed, urgent voice. I couldn't decide if it meant that the Germans were preparing to flee or that they were packing up the camp in preparation for a death march.

We lined up at *appell* the next morning as if nothing had happened. We stood at attention, waiting as the SS officers strode up and down the lines to make sure that nobody was missing. We waited for the signal to be dismissed to work.

The dismissal never came. We continued to stand in our places, nervously wondering what was going on. Were they going to order us to start marching?

One of the girls standing at the end of the line overheard two SS officers talking, and she whispered a name to the girl standing in front of her. The name spread like wildfire through the lines of waiting girls, and a wave of fright followed immediately after. I shuddered violently when Sarah whispered the name in my ear.

Hauptmann! Hauptmann was coming! It could only mean bad news. Hauptmann was the leader of all the concentration camps in the Halbstadt area. If he was coming to our camp, something terrible was about to happen.

He had been at our camp only a few days before, administering punishment to the hapless girl who had been caught with a pencil and paper. Instead of the execution we had all expected, he had ordered one of the Nazis to give her twenty-five lashes with a leather whip. Was he coming back to order her death? Or could it be something worse?

A long, black car drove up. None of us moved as the door slowly opened and Hauptmann got out of the car. We stood perfectly still as he walked up to us. I felt a curious thought intruding into my state of panic. Where were his dogs? Hauptmann was always escorted by two huge, black dogs that slavered with eagerness at the sight of so many victims. We had never seen him without their company, but now he was standing in front of us alone.

He swallowed hard. Instead of holding his head high and looking down his nose at us as he usually did, his eyes were downcast and his shoulders were slumped. He cleared his throat several times before he managed to speak.

"You," he said hoarsely, "my dear, dear children." It was

a tremendous effort for him to talk to us in such a civil manner. "You are going . . . home now. The war is over. You are free." He seemed to choke over the word. "You have a future." With shaking hands, he ripped off all the medals glittering on his uniform and threw them on the ground. The proud, arrogant Hauptmann stood before us, humble and crushed. "You have a future, but as for me, I don't know." He started to cry as he turned away from us and began to walk to his car.

No one moved. Five hundred girls just stood there and let a murderer walk away. All of the SS officers had disappeared during Hauptmann's speech; there were no guards, no guns trained on us, nothing to stop us from pouncing on that hated man and ripping him to shreds. Yet we stood there and watched him walk away. Something held us back from sinking to that final level of murder. Perhaps it was our final act of defiance. We showed that Nazi that, unlike the Germans, a Jew always behaves like a human being, no matter what the circumstances.

It was May 8, 1945. Sarah and I were free.

# CHAPTER 25

■

# The Peasant Woman

N OW THAT WE WERE LIBERATED FROM OUR SLAVERY, Sarah and I were eager to find our father and become a family again. Before we left the area, however, we both wanted to find the peasant woman and thank her for all she had done for us. We owed her so much, and we didn't want to leave without telling her how much we appreciated her sensitivity and concern.

I spent the next afternoon standing together with Sarah right outside the closed Schrohl textile factory, hoping that our benefactor would show up so we could thank her. The shadows lengthened and the sun began to set, but there was no sign of the one-eyed peasant woman who had saved us from starvation. Neither of us had any idea what her name was, much less where she lived. We had no way of finding her.

The next morning, Sarah and I walked into Halbstadt to make inquiries about the peasant woman. Most of the houses were empty; many of the Germans had fled from the advancing Russians. We stopped people on the road, describing the woman and asking them if they knew her, but nobody seemed to know who we were talking about. We were both feeling very discouraged. In the late afternoon, when we were just about ready to return to the camp empty-handed, we stopped a young girl and asked her if she knew our peasant woman. We were surprised by her warm response. The girl told us that she knew the woman well; she lived about twelve kilometers away from our camp. She gave us basic directions and walked away.

I was so excited that I had a hard time falling asleep that night. Before dawn, Sarah and I were already on our way towards our friend's cottage, eager to see her again and thank her for all she had done for us.

The sun was high in the sky by the time we reached the peasant woman's home. It was more a hut than a house, a tiny building with a thatched roof and a single window and door. There was no path or steps; it was just a little hut standing in the middle of nowhere. Sarah and I exchanged surprised glances. We hadn't known what to expect, but we were surprised to see such obvious poverty. Summoning up my courage, I knocked at the door.

"*Hereinkommen!*" answered a hoarse voice. I felt a surge of excitement. I recognized the voice I had only heard once before, on the very first day when she had entered the factory. I gently opened the door, and the two of us walked in.

She was there, bending over her open stove as she concentrated on lighting the fire. She turned around and saw us. Her face lit up, and she ran over and hugged me tightly.

It was a long time since anyone had cared enough to give me a hug, and I couldn't stop tears from springing into my eyes.

She was so pleased to see me, even though she didn't understand how I had managed to find her. I related the events of the past few days and introduced her to Sarah. She grasped Sarah by the shoulders, looked her up and down and gave a little sob.

"Such a child!" she said as she hugged Sarah. "Such a child!"

She had us sit down and share her lunch. She gave us each a sandwich; one slice of white bread, one slice of black and a thick slab of white cheese. It was the lunch she ate every single day, and she had shared what little she had with us for seven full months. She was obviously very poor; all she had was an iron bed, a rickety table with two chairs, an oven and some pots and pans. She insisted that we sit on the chairs; she ate her lunch sitting on the bed. She watched us intently as we ate. I found my eyes filling with tears again. She had so little, and she was so willing to give! It was unbelievable to discover that there were actually Germans who were kindhearted and decent.

Hesitantly, I started to thank her for all she had done for us, but she wouldn't let me finish talking. She felt she had done what was necessary and there was nothing more to be said. She stood up rather abruptly and told us to follow her. Sarah and I, feeling slightly bewildered, followed her out of the hut and down the road.

We arrived at a luxurious home, where our friend introduced us to the lady of the house. In seconds, we were whisked into the dining room and seated at a huge table covered with a lovely embroidered cloth. We dazedly accepted the coffee and cake that was offered to us. I hadn't seen food like that in almost six years, and I couldn't quite believe that I was sitting in an elegant dining room and sipping hot coffee out of a delicate china cup.

Our hostess presented each of us with a dress before allowing us to leave. Sarah and I were overwhelmed by the grace and kindness these people were showing us. We thanked our hostess as graciously as we could and left the house, ready to return to our camp. Our friend insisted on escorting us back to camp, saying that she did not want us walking alone in the dark.

As we bid her farewell outside our barracks, I found myself thinking that if only a few more gentiles would have been as kind as this one-eyed peasant woman, many more Jews would have managed to survive the war. How many Jews had been betrayed to the Nazis by their conniving neighbors? All the Poles who had cooperated so eagerly with the Nazis were as guilty as the Germans were, I thought bitterly. I bowed my head, thinking of those that had failed to outlive the war. Sarah, who seemed to know what I was thinking, slowly touched my hand.

"Tomorrow," she said softly. "Tomorrow we will start looking for Tatteshe."

# CHAPTER 26

■

## Searching for Father

W E STARTED OUT WITH HIGH HOPES. SURELY OUR father had survived the war! How many times had I felt as if he was looking over my shoulder, calmly encouraging me to continue the struggle to live in the face of death? I was confident that we would be able to find him and become a family once more.

We found out that there was a concentration camp for men just eight kilometers away from Halbstadt, so we started from there. The camp was a small one; there were only eight hundred men. We spent a whole day talking to the men there, describing our father and asking if anyone had seen him. Unfortunately, nobody was able to help us; both the name and description seemed to be completely unfamiliar to the men in the camp. Several men looked at us with expressions of compassion as they gently warned us that the chances of finding our father was very slim. Undaunted, we asked if there was another camp nearby; we were given directions to a very large camp called Schathausen, about thirty kilometers away.

After a sleepless night, Sarah and I set out for Schathausen. I was still very optimistic. I was confident that Hashem had allowed Tatteshe to survive the war. Sarah seemed more anxious, but she kept her misgivings to herself.

There was no public transportation available, so walking was our only method of travel. We walked from village to village, tramping along in the heat of the day. My feet became dreadfully swollen, and we had to stop often to rest. We hadn't reached our destination by the time night fell, so we ended up sleeping in the grass by the side of the road.

Early the next morning, Sarah and I were on our way again. We were delighted to see a wagon approaching us on the road, and we ran forward eagerly to ask for a ride. The driver allowed us to sit in the back of the wagon. We clambered aboard gratefully, relieved at the chance to stay off our feet for a little while.

As the wagon rumbled along the dirt road, Sarah idly scanned the countryside. Suddenly, she sat up and pointed at a man walking in the fields. His gaunt looks marked him as a *muselman,* one of the walking skeletons that came out of the concentration camps more dead than alive. Calling our thanks to the driver, we clambered down from the wagon and ran to speak to the *muselman.* Perhaps he would have some information for us.

The *muselman* told us that we were near Schathausen, the terrible death camp where thousands had been killed.

"There are still some people alive over there," he said

199

slowly. "There is also a register of all the six million Jews who were killed by the Nazis. You might be able to find your father's name on the register."

Six million! We stared at him in horror. Six million Jews! It was the first time we had ever heard a specific number. My mind reeled at the thought. Six million dead!

Sarah started to cry. She no longer believed that we would find Tatteshe alive. I couldn't understand her. Of course our father was still alive! He was young, he was healthy; he had a tremendous will to live. I stubbornly insisted that we would find Tatteshe alive and well.

We started walking again. A little while later, a truck driver offered us a ride. We sat silently in the cab of the truck, each of us lost in thought. One hour later, we were at the gates of Schathausen.

The place was a living nightmare. There were piles of dead bodies—two stories high! The people stumbling around looked as if they had risen from the pile of the dead; their eyes were lifeless and their bodies little more than mere skeletons. As we stood there transfixed by the horrible sight, I saw three or four *muselmen* quietly collapse. They died, just like that; they didn't even realize they had been liberated.

There was a small wooden shack about fifty feet away from us, its entrance wide open. People were sitting on the ground inside the shack, leafing through the pages of gigantic books. Most of them were crying. I realized these people had come to Schathausen on the same errand as us, trying to find out what had happened to the members of their family. It seemed obvious that almost all of them had been disappointed.

Sarah simply looked at me. All my confidence and hope seemed to evaporate in an instant. Hashem, please, let us find proof that Tatteshe is still alive!

We entered the crowded shack and gave our names to a secretary. He handed me a heavy book and told me to look through it for my father's name. I sat down on the floor with Sarah at my side and opened the book. The book had names in it, hundreds and hundreds of pages of names. I found myself trembling at the sheer volume of names. All these people were dead! All the millions of names in these books were people who had been killed for the sin of being a Jew.

As I slowly turned the pages of the huge volume, I noticed that several names were not marked off as dead; instead, the book noted when that person had been through Schathausen. Most of the names also had a date of death next to them, but there were a small number of people whose date of death had not been written down. I clung to the small hope that Tatteshe's name would be one of them.

I was afraid to turn to the letter L. Sarah, sitting next to me, seemed to understand my reluctance. What would we do if we found our father's name written down, with the date of death stamped next to his name? I found myself turning the pages more and more slowly, putting off the dreaded moment of truth.

Suddenly, Tatteshe's name leaped out at me. I gave a little scream, and Sarah grabbed my arm in a panic. I pointed wordlessly at the name, and Sarah peered closely at the page. It was our father's name, with his date of birth written next to it. And right next to that . . .

I sighed with relief. *Baruch Hashem!* There was no date of death written in the register. The only other information given was that on February 17, 1945, our father had passed through Schathausen.

I found myself half-laughing with relief. I hugged Sarah

impulsively, babbling with excitement. When Sarah did not return the embrace, I looked at her face, startled to see that her cheeks were wet with tears.

"Why are you crying now?" I asked, puzzled. "Don't you see? Tatteshe was alive a few months ago! If he survived until then, he must be alive now! Why, he's probably back in Lodz already. All we have to do is go back to our apartment, and we'll be united again!"

Sarah said nothing. She slowly looked away, towards the piles of dead bodies and the *muselmen* who had collapsed. Tears glittered on her face, but she didn't say a word.

# CHAPTER 27

———————◼———————

# The Journey Home

THE ROAD TO LODZ WAS A LONG ONE, AND WE HAD NO means of transportation. We walked along the road, accepting rides in trucks, jeeps and horse-drawn wagons. It was an exhausting trip, but we were buoyed by the hope that we would be united with our father at journey's end.

When we reached Polish soil, we heard that there was a slight possibility of boarding a train. We hurried eagerly towards the nearest train station, about a half day's journey on foot. Sarah and I were excited at the prospect of rapid transportation into Lodz.

When we arrived at the station, our chances of boarding a train looked very slim. The place was packed, and some people were complaining that they had been waiting for over

SISTERS IN THE STORM

two days. Sarah, however, suggested to me that if two days had already passed without a train, there was a strong chance of a train coming in to the station within the next day or so. I conceded the point, and the two of us settled down to wait.

As the night wore on, the two of us found ourselves moving toward the back of the station almost against our will. More and more people were streaming into the station, and the pressure of so many people pushing and shoving was carrying us closer and closer to the tracks. In a way, that was good; it meant that we had a greater chance of boarding the train when it finally came. At any rate, I no longer thought it feasible to leave the station and continue our journey on foot, since there was no way we could have fought our way through the crowd to get out.

It was late afternoon on the following day when the train finally groaned its way into the station. The crowd, which had been unruly enough until then, erupted into a madhouse. I never heard so many curses in one place in so many different languages in my life, much less had I seen so many fists and elbows in motion. Sarah and I were pushed and pummelled in every which way, and getting on board the train seemed absolutely hopeless.

A quiet voice in Sarah's ear startled her. A young Russian soldier looked at her inquiringly, gesturing toward the train. It was obvious that he was offering to help her get on board. Sarah nodded eagerly, pointing at me to show that the two of us were together. Neither of us spoke Russian, so we were unable to communicate properly with him.

It didn't seem to matter. The soldier flashed us a brief grin before pursing his lips and letting out a shrill whistle. Another Russian came striding forward, and the two soldiers ostentatiously helped us board the train. The Poles milling around fell back, unwilling to argue with two of the liberators of Poland. Russian soldiers were held in very deep respect for their part in the victory over Germany, and in seconds, Sarah and I were seated comfortably on the train, delighted by the sudden turn of events.

As the train pulled out of the station, the two soldiers sat down next to us—much too close for comfort. As time passed, we realized uncomfortably that they expected us to show our appreciation for their assistance. Sarah and I eyed each other. The years of terror we had been through together had taught us how to communicate without speaking, and we silently agreed to disappear from the train at the first available opportunity.

When the train stopped at the next station, we smiled as sweetly as possible at our "benefactors" and motioned in the direction of the washroom. We walked to the back of the car and quickly ducked out the entrance. Moving hurriedly, we made our way through the noisy crowd towards the front of the train. Sure enough, we saw one of the soldiers lean out the window and scan the crowd, a large scowl on his face. We edged behind the tallest man we could find, hoping the Russian wouldn't notice us. *Baruch Hashem,* the train departed without any further incident. We were sorry to lose our easy mode of transportation, but we were relieved to get away from the two Russian soldiers.

Sarah and I sat on the ground, waiting for another train to arrive. The station was near a small village, and very few trains passed through. I overheard someone say that there would only be freight trains carrying coal, and I wondered how we could possibly get any use out of a freight train.

After several hours, a freight train pulled into the station. I eyed it, trying to figure out a way to get on board. Sarah, however, had already come up with a plan. She swarmed up the small ladder on the side of one of the cars and scrambled over the gravelly coal, settling herself into a small hollow. I quickly followed her. The two of us managed to scoop away some of the coal and make a kind of seat for ourselves. We were both already covered with black dust, but I was delighted to be on another train going in the right direction.

As we sat on our perch high above the station, the train began to move. Our smiles of satisfaction quickly vanished when the coal began to shift and slide underneath us. We ended up lying flat on our stomachs, hugging the coal in an attempt to avoid sliding off the train completely. It was nerve-wracking, but I'll always remember Sarah's grin, her white teeth flashing in a face blackened with soot. I smiled back. It was good to be free and travelling, no matter how awkwardly, toward Lodz and our father.

The light was beginning to fade when the train finally arrived at Lodz. Sarah and I made our way down the ladder, happy to be at our destination. Now we would finally be reunited with our father!

As confident as I wanted to feel, I still had to confront reality. What if our father was not waiting for us? What if Tatteshe was dead? The last few months before the liberation had been the bloodiest, with the Nazis trying to erase all evidence of their systematic genocide. Had our father managed to survive?

Our first step was to go to the Yiddishe Gemino, a center where all Jewish survivors registered their names. The idea was to have one place where people could go to find out if the members of their family were in the city. We walked through the deserted streets, uncomfortable at the lack of any sign of life. Lodz, which had literally vibrated with Jewish life before the war, seemed empty and dead. I felt like an outsider in a foreign city, walking through streets unfamiliar and strange.

We arrived at the Gemino. There were several people there, but the atmosphere was hushed and subdued. Aside from the register, the walls were scribbled with signatures in Yiddish, Polish and German, messages left behind by people in the hopes that relatives had survived the war and would be able to read them. The names and dates scrawled on the wall were a poignant reminder that we were only one of thousands of families that had been torn apart during the war. Each name was a silent witness to the suffering our people had undergone in the last several years.

Sarah and I spent a full day there, just reading the walls. We were terribly disappointed to discover that our father's name was not among those that decorated the walls, but we refused to give up. We came back the next day, approaching any person that looked vaguely familiar. We asked if the person had seen Tatteshe, describing him in detail. Not a single person was able to help us; they either shook their heads or shrugged their shoulders. No one had seen him or knew anything about him.

We spent an entire week there, searching and inquiring. We slept in a small room designated for travellers along with dozens of others. We made one side trip to the Jewish cemetery to visit the graves of Mammeshe and Binyamin. We were puzzled by eight huge graves that lay open to the sky; there seemed to be no reason for them at all.

Finally, we decided it was time to go to our old apartment and see if there was any message there. I felt a great deal of reluctance. The apartment seemed to be our last hope, and I was afraid of what we might find there.

I had a hard time keeping my emotions under control as

we approached the intersection of Pilsudskeigo and Kammienna Street. The physical appearance of our old neighborhood was unchanged; there was no destruction, no ruins, no shattered buildings. The streets, sidewalks, traffic, stores, houses and courtyards were all the same. It was as if this section of Lodz was unaware that there had been a war for six years. People stood in doorways, laughing and talking, while children played in the courtyards. I shook myself. The whole thing seemed so unreal!

The gateway to our courtyard stood wide open, as it always had been at this time of day. Karol, our superintendent, was standing with his large broom in hand and talking to the superintendent of the next house, just as he always used to do. I exchanged looks of disbelief with Sarah. It was as if we had gone back in time to the 1930s, before the war even began!

Sarah nudged me. She pointed towards the three windows of our apartment. I followed her gaze and saw the same pastel-colored curtains my mother had sewn fluttering in the stiff breeze.

One look at those beloved, familiar curtains sent me hurtling back in time, to a moment before the war when I had been innocent, happy and carefree. It was *Erev Pesach,* and Mammeshe had just finished hanging up the curtains she had sewn *l'kavod Yom Tov.* The sun filtered through the curtains to pick up the glistening shine of the polished floor, and the entire apartment sparkled with the cleanliness and freshness of *Pesach.*

The *seder* that night . . . My father in his lovely, embroidered *kittel,* his face aglow as he sat at the head of the table. Both of my grandfathers were there, beaming with pride. My mother sat demurely at her place at the table, satisfied with her beautiful *seder* table. My father smiled at his *aishes chayil,* his woman of valor, who has done the impossible with her usual flair. My mother in her green satin dress ... We children dressed in our very best, with the little bows and ribbons lovingly sewn on to our clothing to make us look even nicer. My father lifting his *kiddush* cup, preparing to start the *Pesach seder* . . .

A tugging at my sleeve snapped me out of my reverie. Sarah was saying something. I blinked and shook myself, realizing for the first time that a stranger was peeking at us from behind the curtains of our apartment. He looked angry and suspicious. Sarah and I looked nervously at each other before mounting the steps to knock on the door and explain ourselves.

"Who is it?" The voice was hoarse and unfamiliar. When neither of us answered, the door opened a crack, just enough for the man to see our faces. He squinted at us warily. "What do you want?" he demanded.

I was unable to answer. I was staring past him, looking at our furniture and our pictures hanging on the wall. Nothing was moved; nothing had changed; and yet nothing was the same. I stared, mesmerized, until I was rudely awakened by the slamming of the door in our faces. I looked blankly at the closed door for several moments before turning away. Groping for Sarah's hand, the two of us stumbled down the stairs, our hearts broken.

Outside in the courtyard, Karol was absentmindedly sweeping the ground. He stopped when he saw us. His face looked as if he had just seen a ghost. He quickly crossed himself.

"You're still alive?" he exclaimed. "Why, I thought you

had died long ago! But why are you here? What do you want here?"

We walked past without answering. There didn't seem to be anything to say.

As we walked into the street and around the corner, the whole thing seemed to crash down on us all at once. We simultaneously burst into tears, holding on to each other for support. After several minutes, we wiped each other's tears and slowly resumed walking. But where? We had no place to go. The home of our childhood was gone; our family had vanished; our last hope of reunion had faded away. We walked for several minutes in silence, wandering aimlessly through the streets; then we stopped and turned to each other.

"Sarah," I began.

"Chanka," Sarah said at the same time.

And together, we asked each other, "Where is Tatteshe now?"

# CHAPTER 27

---■---

## Lodgings

W E HAD NOWHERE TO GO, SO WE JUST WANDERED UP and down the streets of our childhood. The light began to fade, but we didn't have a place to sleep or money with which to buy food; so we roamed the streets at random, in a state of apathy close to that which we had undergone in the labor camp. We knew we would never see Tatteshe again, and we felt lost and forlorn in our own town. The war seemed to have passed everyone else by; people laughed and strolled through the streets at their leisure, buying goods and groceries at whim. How did they have money? Where did they get currency? It hadn't dawned on us that Lodz had been liberated months before we had been, and the war was that much further away from the towns-people. We felt resentful of these people that were seemingly oblivious to our misery.

As we turned onto one of the main streets of Lodz, I smelled an aroma I had forgotten long, long ago. I stood still and breathed deeply, inhaling the wonderful smell of fresh cake. We were approaching a bakery, and the wonderful smells wafting out of the open door were almost more than I could stand. Without thinking, I found myself walking into the store and pressing my nose against the glass display cabinets. Rolls, loaves of bread, danishes, doughnuts, cakes. I was entranced by a world of food that I hadn't seen for over six years.

The bakery was doing a brisk business. Customers filled the shop, buying cakes, rolls and bread. Everyone seemed to have plenty of money to spend. I shrank back into a corner and devoured the whole scene with hungry eyes.

Suddenly, I realized that the lady standing behind the counter was speaking to me. Startled, I looked up. I realized that all the other customers had left and I was the only one in the store.

"I'm sorry, I didn't hear you," I apologized.

"I asked you what you wanted to buy," said the woman with a quizzical look on her face.

I looked down and shuffled my feet. "I don't have any money," I mumbled. I wanted to sink into the floor in shame.

She looked at me for a long moment before bending down and taking two danishes out of the display case. She wrapped them in a piece of paper and handed me the little package.

I looked at the package, desperately wanting to take it. "I-I said that I have no money," I repeated hesitantly.

"Take it," she said with a sad smile. "Take it, *mein kind,* and enjoy it."

I felt my knees start to tremble. Part of me wanted to turn on my heel and proudly walk away, but the temptation was much too great. I was still finding it very hard to cope with kindness. I was much too used to kicks, beatings and sadism. Her face blurred as I blinked back my tears. I slowly stretched out my hand and took the package. I whispered a thank you without looking at the woman and shuffled out of the store, clutching the precious package with both hands.

Outside, Sarah was talking to a strange young man. He had evidently realized that we had just arrived in Lodz from a concentration camp. He was asking her if she was lacking food or clothing. As I moved to join them, the young man asked Sarah if we had a place to stay for the night. When she told him that we didn't, he simply picked up our bundles and told us to follow him.

We looked at him with astonishment as he strode off with what was left of our possessions. We ran after him, more for the sake of our things than the possibility of shelter for the night. However, when he reached his apartment and started to fit his key in the lock, Sarah and I remembered the Russian soldiers on the train. We wondered uneasily if this young man had the same thing in mind. The two of us slowly backed away, getting ready to run.

The young man noticed our anxiety and tried to reassure us. "It's all right," he said with a smile. "I understand. Listen, you don't have to stay with me. My friend across the hall has three girls sleeping in the back room of his apartment. Maybe you'll feel more comfortable there." He moved across the hall and banged on a door. "Hey, Kozak!" he yelled. "There are some girls from Lodz who just got back from the camps. Let them in!"

A tall, gangly man opened the door, with three girls

peering over his shoulder. The kind look on his thin face did more to relieve us than anything else. He invited us in, showing us into the back room where we could put our things. Conversation revealed that he was the first cousin of some friends of ours. The three girls were obviously *frum*, and I found myself slowly relaxing for the first time in days.

Kozak told us that he was one of the people chosen to clean up the ghetto after the final liquidation. Sarah and I exchanged puzzled glances.

"Have you been to the cemetery since your return?" he asked us in his quiet voice.

"Yes, we have," I replied.

"Did you notice the large open graves?"

"Yes. What were they from?"

"We dug them—for ourselves." He paused for a moment, looking down at his hands. "Sixty thousand people were deported to Auschwitz in the last two months of the summer of 1944. There were only eight hundred of us left, and we were ordered to clean up the ghetto. We went from house to house, removing the dead. We cleaned the streets . . ." His voice trailed off, and I knew he must be reliving those terrible moments, gathering together the dead bodies of people he had known and loved. "When we were finished, they took us to the cemetery and told us to dig our own graves."

Sarah and I shuddered.

Kozak smiled slightly at our reaction before he continued his tale. "They were very specific about it," he said. "Eight graves, they told us. Each one should be seven feet long, seven feet wide, and five feet deep. By the time we finished with the job, it was already dark. We expected to be ordered to line up at the edge of the graves, but they locked us up in the memorial hall instead. We figured that they wanted a little extra fun with us, so we all resolved not to beg for mercy when the time came."

I nodded. This was something I could understand, the desire to cheat the Nazis of as much satisfaction as possible, the refusal to lose our dignity in the face of all that they did to us.

"None of us could believe it when we saw the sun rise the next morning. We had all expected to be dead long before that." Kozak sighed. "But nothing happened. We spent the entire day locked in the memorial hall. The Nazis had all disappeared. After nightfall, we were released by a contingent of Russian soldiers." Kozak looked at us with a strange expression on his face. "Just think! I owe my life to Nazi sadism. If they hadn't been so determined to make us suffer for another night, we would have died a day before Lodz was liberated by the Russians."

Sarah and I were silent. We were awed by the story Kozak had told us. After several minutes, Kozak got up and told us he was leaving for the night. He put on a ragged coat, nodded at the five of us, and left the apartment, closing the door behind him.

The three girls, who had remained mostly silent during Kozak's company, jumped up and escorted us into the back room. There were no beds, but they assured us that it wasn't a problem.

"We sleep on the floor, but there's plenty of bedding. Don't worry, you'll be comfortable!" They spoke cheerfully and animatedly, bringing out large blankets, pillows and linen as they chattered to each other. Sarah and I helped them spread the linen out on the floor. Within minutes, the five of us were snuggled underneath our blankets and on the verge of sleep.

As my eyes slowly closed, I realized that it had been five years and ten months since Sarah and I had slept in a regular apartment.

We realized that Kozak was letting us sleep in his apartment while he slept elsewhere, but it was only a temporary arrangement. Sarah and I would have to find more permanent lodgings if we wanted to stay in Lodz.

When Kozak came back to the apartment the next morning, we asked him if he knew about any other girls that had returned to Lodz. He mentioned several names, but none of them were familiar to us. Then, remembering he had said that he was a cousin of Rochelka and Pola Baumac, we asked him if they were safely back in Lodz.

"Of course," he said, surprised. "I should have thought of that myself! They're in an apartment on Pomorska Street."

Sarah and I were pleased at the news. Rochelka had been in the same Bnos group with me, and our families had always been close. Now that I had abandoned hope of being reunited with my family, I was eager to be reunited with old friends.

As the two of us walked briskly towards Pomorska Street, we met Tola Braun, a woman about ten years older than me. She married before the war, but she lost her husband in Auschwitz. She had worked together with us in the Schrohl factory, so we knew her well. The three of us went on together, talking amiably while I tried to hide the gnawing feeling that Rochelka might not recognize us. After all, my hair was a ragged stubble, I was as thin as a rail, and my face reflected all the horrors I had witnessed. Would she see the old Chanka Landman in me?

*Baruch Hashem,* I had worried for nothing! Rochelka was delighted to see us, and she recognized me instantly. After

216

the initial flurry of hugs and tearful laughter, she invited us into the apartment and asked what she could do to help. We explained our housing problem, and her face fell.

"I wish you could stay here!" she said unhappily. "But you see, it's not my apartment. It really belongs to Pola's friend, and she's letting the two of us stay here. Actually, her name is Pola, too, but . . . well, maybe she'll let you stay, and . . . oh, here they are!"

We turned around to see Pola Baumac walk in together with another girl, who turned out to be the other Pola. She expressed regret that she couldn't put us up in the apartment, but she suggested that a neighbor across the courtyard might be able to let us use a room in his spacious apartment. I was disappointed; I had wanted to stay among friends. Still, there was nothing I could do about it, so I decided to make the best of it.

Rochelka, who had walked into the kitchen for a moment, came back into the room, carrying mugs of hot, sweet tea and a plate of bread. We spent the meal telling each other stories of our lives in the concentration camp. Rochelka's older sister Pola seemed to know vivid details about events that had happened at the very beginning of the ghetto. I knew that Lodz Jews had been murdered in Chelmno, but this was the first time I heard that Chelmno had been the very first death camp initiated by the Nazis and that nearly half a million Jews had been put to death there.

The monstrous death factory in Chelmno was opened on December 8, 1941, and remained in operation until January of 1945. The Nazis used various methods to exterminate the Jews unfortunate enough to pass through the gates of the little city, and all of them proved equally effective.

The first wave of murder was done in an almost primitive

217

fashion. About 2,500 Jews were crammed into a church in Chelmno and locked up for three days without food and water. There wasn't even room to sit down; one woman went into labor, and she was forced to give birth standing up. Both mother and baby died of the pain.

The prisoners broke the windows in their desperate need for air to breathe. Those that tried to escape through the windows were either shot or tortured to death. Finally, when the Germans grew bored, they brought the Jews out of the church and marched them into the forest. When the Nazis ordered them to dig pits, they had no idea they were digging their own graves. But when the job was completed, they were all ordered to lie face down in the deep holes, and a storm of machine-gun bullets quickly wiped out the first contingent of victims of the Chelmno death camp.

As the months wore on, the Germans in Chelmno perfected their system. The rumors that the Nazis had so carefully planted among their victims disarmed the Jews and made them think they were safe. The rumors varied; sometimes the Jews heard that Chelmno was to become the new Jewish community for all Jews in Poland, or that they would leave Chelmno and go to other ghettos to work for the Nazis. Everything was designed to keep the victims quiet and docile; as long as the Jews were deceived, they wouldn't interfere with the efficiency of their death.

When a new transport arrived, they were taken to the churches. The walls were scribbled over with messages: "Today's transport of seven hundred Jews was here." "Yesterday, a group of nine hundred people were here from Lodz." "We are being taken to a ghetto in southern Poland." The messages heartened the Jews; they had no idea that the people who wrote the messages had been just as much deceived as they were.

At the church, the Jews were met by Gestapo agents, both in uniform and civilian clothing. The Germans were smiling pleasantly; they actually helped people down from the trucks. The Nazis acted courteously and politely, convincing their victims that they really were going to be taken to another ghetto where the men would have jobs in factories, the women would have jobs as housekeepers, and the children would be sent to schools.

The Jews were told that they should leave their belongings in the church for the moment while they went to the castle to be bathed and disinfected. The "castle" was actually what was left of a much larger strucure which had been bombed during World War I. The Jews followed the Nazis trustingly, entering a large, well-heated room in the castle. The words "Bath Institution" were painted on the walls in large, neat letters. The deception was complete down to the very last detail.

The hapless victims were asked to disrobe in preparation for their baths. "Just leave your clothing here," said a smiling Gestapo officer. "We'll be giving you everything you need. I assure you that you won't need those clothes again!"

The Jews didn't notice the steel lurking beneath the velvet glove. They filed obediently out of the warm, tiled room into a bitterly cold hallway. The looks of bewilderment on their faces quickly changed to expressions of horror as the situation changed completely. With whips and gun butts, the Jews were driven into execution vehicles, solidly built trucks with some chilling additions built in. The net had tightened, and the victims were very neatly caught. Prayers rang through the air, mingling with the sounds of weeping. Too late, the Jews realized that they were being sent to their deaths.

The trucks were used to kill one hundred people at a time.

When the victims had been forced into the truck, the doors were sealed shut. There was no air circulating inside the truck, and the sealed doors prevented any air from getting in, so it took only ten minutes before the people inside began to suffocate. The Nazi driver would indifferently move the truck out of Chelmno into the woods. He stopped near a contingent of SS men and their Jewish prisoners, fifty men who were forced to dig graves for the victims. When the driver saw that the graves were ready, he turned on the gas mechanism. All he had to do was press several buttons on his dashboard to cause gas to flood the back of the truck. The stifled cries and muffled pounding would cease after fifteen minutes, and the Nazis could take satisfaction in another job completed—another hundred Jews dead.

After several minutes, the German drove the truck closer to the open graves. Two of the Jewish gravediggers were ordered to open the back door. A terrible odor of gas flooded the air, forcing the gravediggers back. After a while, when the air had cleared, the gravediggers removed the bodies from the trucks and buried them in the graves. The Nazis examined the bodies first, pulling off rings and using pliers to wrench out any gold teeth.

The gravediggers were often forced to bury their own relatives without any time to mourn. There was no decency, no respect for the dead. The victims were laid in the graves with the feet of one body jammed against the head of another. Any gaps were filled with the bodies of small children. When an entire layer of bodies had been laid down, a thin layer of earth was thrown over the corpses and another tier of corpses was placed in the grave.

The gravediggers didn't last very long. Every few days, the Nazis would order the current gravediggers to lie face down in the graves they had just filled with dead bodies. As the men lay there, bracing themselves for death, an SS officer would riddle their brains with machine gun bullets. Another group of gravediggers would be selected to serve until they, too, were murdered.

The Nazis eventually grew dissatisfied with the death factory. There were complaints that the dead bodies were contaminating the air. The result was the creation of primitive crematoriums to burn the bodies. The bodies were laid out, soaked in benzene and ignited. The ashes were used to fertilize German soil, and the clothing so trustingly left behind in the palace was sorted and sent off to other ghettos. The Germans were pleased with the efficiency of Chelmno. There were never any survivors.

Pola finished the tale by telling the story of forty-five tailors that were left in Chelmno near the end of the war. "The Nazis locked them up," she said darkly. "One of them had tried to escape, so they locked them up in a wooden building and set it ablaze."

"They burned them alive?" gasped Sarah.

"Why are you so surprised?" I asked her bitterly. "Don't you think they're capable of acting like that?"

Sarah looked down, troubled. Rochelka broke the awkward silence by offering to accompany us to their neighbor to see if we could board there for a little while.

Sarah and I spent several weeks shuttling miserably from one room to another. We often stayed together with another girl or two, only to move on for one reason or another. Once, the man who owned the apartment tried to break into our room at night; another time, we left because the girl with whom we stayed suddenly disappeared. We tried going to the police, but they just laughed it off, saying she had run off with a boy. Her body was found near the cemetery several days later.

I became more and more convinced that we should get out of Poland entirely and go to Eretz Yisrael. The mere idea seemed utterly ridiculous; how could two penniless girls manage the long, dangerous trip? Still, I wouldn't let that deter me. I felt sick at the idea of remaining on soil soaked with Jewish blood. I didn't know how I was going to do it, but I became determined to find some way to leave Poland and make my way to Eretz Yisrael.

# CHAPTER 28

◼

## Out of Poland

I T WAS *SHABBOS* NIGHT, BUT THE HOUSE WAS DREARILY empty. I was lost in my thoughts, dreamily remembering happier times before the war. Mammeshe wearing her green silk dress as she lovingly lit the *Shabbos* candles; Tatteshe wearing his long, glossy black *bekeshe*, making *kiddush* over the sparkling red wine; Binyamin, his clear voice lifted in song. The images were so vivid that I actually turned around to see if they were there. The stark, bitter reality that confronted me was too much to take. I threw on my shabby coat and left the apartment.

As I wandered through the streets, it occurred to me that I was right by the new Kibbutz Agudas Yisrael. It was a *frum* organization, a spinoff of Bnos, that was geared towards helping religious girls get to Eretz Yisrael. The term *"kibbutz"* had thrown me off at first; I had always associated the term with the cultivation of land. Actually, in this context, the term simply signified a group of people intent on getting to Eretz Yisrael. The differences between them that are so vast today really did not exist at the time. Only their methods remained different. That night, depressed as I was, I decided to check out the *kibbutz* and see what it was really like.

I'll never forget the sight that greeted my eyes when I walked up the stairs at Zachodnia 66 and opened the door. There were two glowing *Shabbos* candles right next to a bottle of deep red wine, gracing a table covered with a spotless white tablecloth! I stared, entranced. Was I dreaming?

A shout of delight convinced me that I wasn't as Fayga Janowska threw her arms around me in joy. Malka Finkler, a native of Protrkov and a grandchild of the Radyszutzer Rebbe, was the leader of the Agudah Kibbutz in Lodz after the war. She had been in my Bnos group together with Fayga. Together, they urged me to join the *kibbutz* right away and spend *Shabbos* among friends. Tears sprang to my eyes at the thought of a real *Shabbos,* and I raced back to the apartment to get Sarah.

"Sarah!" I shouted as I banged the door wide open. Sarah, who was laying on the bed and reading a book, sat up in surprise. "Sarah, come on! We're joining the *kibbutz!*"

The words tumbled over themselves as I hurriedly explained. Sarah caught my enthusiasm, and the two of us agreed to go to the *kibbutz* early the following morning.

Dawn was just breaking when Sarah and I made our way back to Zachodnia Street. The warmth and *Yiddishkeit* impressed us so much that we ended up staying the entire *Shabbos.* My throat ached at the beauty of the *zemiros,* the likes of which I hadn't heard in so many years. Even the sound of laughter was something new and fresh, something I had thought I would never hear again. I was so happy that I made up my mind on the spot—I was going to join the *kibbutz!*

Yechiel Granatstein, Malka's *chassan,* made *Havdalah* for us when *Shabbos* was over. Sarah and I said a temporary good-bye to our friends before returning to the apartment for the night. The next morning, we stuffed our few belongings into our knapsacks and left the apartment forever as we went to join the *kibbutz.*

The *kibbutz* had little in the way of material wealth, but its spiritual riches seemed endless. Simply living among religious Jews was a joy in itself! We had an abundance of kosher food, a proper setting for *Shabbos* and the opportunity to learn and grow. It didn't matter that Sarah and I slept on two cots in a room crammed with over two dozen beds; it was of no importance that most of the girls worked at menial tasks to bring in some money for the collective group. The knowledge that we were with *frum* people made all other problems pale into insignificance.

A great deal of emphasis was put on our education. Although Agudas Yisrael had started the *kibbutz* only two months ago, classes had already been set up on a steady basis. We learned *Navi* twice a week, in addition to *Pirkei Avos, parshas hashavua* and *biur tefillah.* We were also taught English as well as current events. The wealth of knowledge I was given helped revitalize my determination to get on with my life.

Although most girls were content to work in the kitchen or iron shirts for their upkeep, I was dissatisfied with such tasks. I was determined to find a job that would be fulfilling and pay a decent salary. Sarah was rather skeptical, but to her surprise (and mine!), I managed to find a job in the office of

225

a textile company. The pay was good, the working conditions were excellent, and my fellow workers were wonderful people. My task was to examine fabrics for flaws in the material. I was free to work at my own pace and be as meticulous as possible. I was delighted with my job, as it was both satisfying and fulfilling.

One particular worker in the textile factory struck a chord deep within me. He was a young tailor, strong, handsome and talented. But it wasn't his beautiful voice that enchanted me; it was the intense concentration with which I saw him put on his *tallis* and *tefillin*. Something healed inside me when I watched him, a festering sore that had been eating away at my heart. Yes, religious people still existed! I watched with awe as he *davened* with intense *kavanah* every morning. I knew from the few words we had exchanged that he had lost his young wife and baby son in the war, and yet he remained so steadfast in his faith in Hashem. This one man convinced me that it was possible to return to our way of life before the war and to continue to live as Jews.

He never told me his name, but the young tailor whose *emunah* in Hashem never faltered will always remain one of the few bright spots in my memories of Poland.

The main intention of the *kibbutz* was to enable its members to reach the shores of Eretz Yisrael. Two weeks after I joined, the first transport of girls left with Aliya Bet, an illegal emigration enterprise. We all knew that it was dangerous, but that didn't stop us from envying the lucky girls who were getting out of Poland and making their way towards Eretz Yisrael. We made them a spirited going-away party, each of us secretly wishing that we were among the chosen few that were leaving. It was very hard to await patiently the time when we would be able to leave Europe for shores that

226

weren't tainted with Jewish blood!

Finally, I heard the good news—Sarah and I had our names down for the next transport! Somehow, the knowledge made the waiting even more difficult. I lay awake nights, formulating endless plans to cover every possible eventuality. I had an obsessive fear of losing my shoes; perhaps it was a holdover from my arrival in Auschwitz, when a lost shoe nearly resulted in my death. I found myself buying another pair of shoes and an extra pair of soles. Sarah took my fixations in stride, although she also found it difficult to cope with the constant postponements of our trip.

Finally, in early September of 1945, we were told to make ourselves ready. We packed what little possessions we had and received our instructions. We met with Shimon Cukier, the head of our section of the *kibbutz*. He gave each girl two hundred *zlotys* and a false identification card. I don't remember my alias, but I was a Greek subject "returning" to Salonika, Greece, from Poland. Our two transport leaders, Yossel Baum and Leibel Zamosc, introduced themselves and gave us some final instructions. As we left the *kibbutz* that night, I could hardly believe that I was leaving Lodz forever, that I would never step foot in Poland again.

# CHAPTER 30

■

## Trouble with Trains

W E MADE OUR WAY TO THE TRAIN STATION, AN
undercurrent of excitement running through
the entire group. Nobody had very much with
them—I had a knapsack on my back and a small suitcase in my
hand—but the knowledge that we were beginning our journey to Eretz Yisrael made us feel richer than kings. It was all
I could do to keep from singing as we went along. I knew it
was going to be dangerous, but I was so happy to be leaving
Poland that I ignored that aspect of our trip entirely.

The station was humming with people when we arrived.
Our group sat on the ground, waiting for the train to arrive.
I found myself remembering the hectic journey to Lodz with
Sarah and our frightening experiences on the trains. I hoped
that this trip would be a little less exciting.

The whistle sounded in the distance, heralding the train's arrival. As the train appeared around the curve of the tracks, the crowds of people surged in the direction of the train. Nobody bothered to wait until the train actually came to a halt. By the time I reached the train myself, it was already packed to capacity.

I had lost sight of Sarah, but I knew she was somewhere nearby. I scrambled onto a narrow platform in between two cars. I peered into the door of the car ahead of me, trying to see if I could spot anyone else from the group. I picked out a few girls and some of the boys sitting together in the middle of the car. Heartened by the knowledge that there were others close by, I tried to find a comfortable spot to lean against. I knew that my trip wasn't going to be comfortable; there was no place to sit on the little platform, and I was going to be exposed to the wind. Still, I was grateful to be on the train at all! The crowds of people milling about on the ground made me realize it was vastly preferable to have an uncomfortable trip than to have no trip at all.

As I leaned against the outside of the door, I heard someone call my name. I turned to see Malka Finkler standing a few feet away from the train, waving as she tried to catch my attention. Malka grabbed my hand and hoisted herself up onto the platform next to me.

"Just wanted to say good-bye, Chanka," she said as she gave me a quick hug. "*Tzaischen l'shalom!* I hope you arrive in safety!" She glanced down at the suitcase I was holding. "Why don't you take off your knapsack and put it down? There's no reason you should be *shlepping* your suitcase, either." She pulled the suitcase out of my hand and set it down on the platform. "You can use it as a seat," she suggested. "That way, you won't have to stand the whole time."

We were interrupted by the conductor, who eyed us suspiciously. It was obvious that he didn't like the idea of having a passenger hanging on the platform outside the cars.

"There is ample space in the front cars," he told me in a disapproving voice. "Why don't you go there?"

Pleased at the idea of actually getting *inside* the train, I hopped off the platform and headed for the front of the train. Malka was right behind me, still carrying my suitcase. We had taken perhaps a half dozen steps when the shrill whistle pierced the air again, and the train began to move.

For one heart-stopping second, I stared with dumbfounded horror at the train, which was slowly picking up speed. Then, without stopping to think, I jumped onto the small ledge running the length of the car, holding onto a small metal bar for dear life. Malka, still holding my suitcase, started running after me, shouting. The train was moving quickly by now, and I clamped my hands down on the bar, grimly determined not to fall and get killed.

"Chanka!" I could still hear Malka calling. "Chanka, your suitcase! What should I do with . . ."

Her voice faded into the distance as the train pulled out of the station, leaving her far behind. All I could concentrate on was not letting go of that bar. The knapsack on my back wasn't helping; I felt as if it was weighing me down, pulling me away from the train. I was terrified that my feet would slip off the ledge, leaving me dangling by the bar for a split second before I lost my grip and fell off the train.

Memories of stories of people jumping off the trains that were transporting them to Auschwitz flashed through my mind. Some of them had managed to survive the fall, but others had not.

I closed my eyes and prayed. My body was swaying

violently with the motion of the train, and the wind was threatening to tear my hands away from the bar. Please, Hashem, I thought, please don't let me die, please.

Suddenly, a hand grabbed my arm. I was so startled that I almost lost my grip. Looking upwards, I saw a boy leaning precariously out of the window right above my head.

"Let go!" he screamed. "Let go of the bar!"

I couldn't do it. My fingers felt like clamps, fastened permanently to the one thing that was my lifeline. There was no way I could let go of the bar. I shook my head at him, my eyes tearing in the fierce wind.

"I can't," I wailed.

"Let go!" he shouted fiercely. "Let go, hurry!"

I knew I couldn't hold on much longer. It was a choice of either slipping to my death or trusting the boy to manage to pull me up. I sent one last plea heavenward, then gritting my teeth, I squeezed my eyes tightly shut and let go of the bar. A strong jerk on my arm pulled me upwards, and then I was sprawled on my back in the laps of three girls, my rescuer standing over me and grinning with relief. I don't know where that boy got the strength to pull me up like that, but it was the first time I was glad that I had lost so much weight over the war years.

The other passengers were clapping, cheering and laughing at the episode. I was too shaken to do anything but gratefully take the seat I was offered by one of the boys from my group. One of the girls helped me pull off my knapsack as I collapsed, trembling violently, into the seat. The whole thing had taken no more than two or three minutes, but I felt as if I had aged a lifetime.

As my breathing slowed down to a normal pace, it dawned on me that half of my clothes and all my food had been left behind in Lodz in the suitcase Malka had been carrying for me. I was relieved to be on board, but I was dismayed to realize that I had no food for the trip at all. There was nothing I could do about it, but I felt so grateful just to be alive! I settled myself deeper into the seat and tried to relax.

I woke up several hours later when the train came to a stop in the middle of a corn field. We all dragged ourselves off the train. I was dazed from sleep and the aftermath of my frightening ordeal, so I merely sat on the grass and did nothing. It was a beautiful, sunny day, but I was too drained to notice.

Someone sat down right next to me. Listlessly, I turned my head and saw Pola sitting on the ground, busily opening her suitcase. She pulled out a roll, broke it in half and handed part of it to me.

"*Nu,* Chanka? Eat!"

I hesitated. I was really hungry, but I didn't want to take any of Pola's food. Noting my hesitation, Pola laughed at me, that irresistible, contagious giggle of hers that was simply impossible to ignore.

"Take it, Chanka," she laughed. "If you don't eat it, it will eat you!"

It sounded ridiculous, but I found myself laughing together with her as I took the roll. I ate it hungrily, sitting with my back to the sun as I talked with Pola. When I tried to thank her, she brushed my thanks away. "Don't be silly, Chanka. It's not a big deal. I know you'd do the same for me. Now stop feeling sorry for yourself and eat!" I obeyed her, smiling to myself as I realized once again just how precious friendship can be.

Immersed in my thoughts, I was startled by the whistle of

the arriving train. Slinging my knapsack over my shoulder, I gave Pola a hand up from the ground, and the two of us boarded the train together.

*Baruch Hashem,* the next stage of my journey was much less eventful. When the train stopped in Cracow, we got off and joined another group of girls from the villages of Bendin and Sosnowice. Together, we boarded another train that took us to Tarnow, where we continued on to Dziedzice.

The dizzying succession of train stops and changes left me bewildered and exhausted, so I was somewhat relieved that the Dziedzice station was a checkpoint. Leibel and Yossel went inside the station to present our papers while we waited outside.

We were a large group by now—close to seventy boys and girls—and we attracted many curious stares from the passersby. Not only were we just sitting there, but our appearances differed drastically from those of the inquisitive Poles that were staring at us. Our hair, shaved off in Auschwitz, was short; we were emaciated and nervous-looking, our eyes darting in all directions at once. When compared with the comfortable, well-fed Poles, we stood out as something different and unusual.

Several of the Poles approached to ask us about ourselves. They wanted to know who we were, what our names were, where we were going and so forth. We were in a bit of a quandary, since we were posing as foreigners that wouldn't know Polish, so there was no way for us to answer their questions.

One of the boys hit upon the perfect solution to our problem. When a Polish peasant walked up to him and started asking questions, he smiled pleasantly at the man and shrugged his shoulders.

*"Modeh ani,"* said the boy in an apologetic tone. *"Torah tziva lanu Moshe?"*

The Pole looked at him blankly. He had no idea what the boy was saying. He repeated his question slowly, enunciating each Polish word as clearly as possible.

The boy beamed. *"Velamalshinim al tehi sikvah!"* he exclaimed.

The Pole threw up his hands in disgust and walked away. We were all struggling not to laugh out loud. Only our uncertainties stopped us from giggling outright. We all took our cue from the boy, smiling and answering all the Poles in phrases from *davening.*

*"Shir hamaalos!"* announced one girl with a broad smile.

*"Kol Yisrael yeish lahem cheilek l'olam habah,"* another boy told a Polish teenager in an earnest tone.

*"Ashrei yoshvei veisecha,"* I said very seriously to a Polish woman.

Sarah, who was standing nearby, almost burst out laughing as she told a woman who had just asked her where she was going that *"Veleyerushalayim ircha berachamim tashuv."* Overhearing her, I also had to struggle not to laugh; the phrase she had just quoted meant "and to Jerusalem return with mercy." The whole situation was utterly ridiculous, but we all found it relaxing to have some fun at the expense of the Polish men and women who had cooperated with the Nazis with such eagerness.

"Look!" I heard one peasant woman say to another. "They look just like us. They aren't dark-skinned or anything. I wonder what language that is? What nationality do you think they are?"

"Perhaps they live near China," suggested her friend. "I asked one of the boys his name, and he told me it was *Yikum*

*Purkan.* That sounds Chinese, doesn't it?"

I turned my head away so they wouldn't see my smile. Only the knowledge that we were still on Polish soil kept me from enjoying myself completely.

After several minutes, Leibel and Yossel emerged from the station, triumphantly waving our stamped papers over their heads. Our certificates had been accepted! On to Czechoslovakia—we were through with inspections!

Or so we thought.

# CHAPTER 31

■

# Russian Roulette

W E ALL BOARDED THE TRAIN, CHATTERING EXCIT-edly in Hebrew to each other. As the train chugged out of the station, we were all delighted to know that our certificates had passed inspection and we were now safe. Unfortunately, it wasn't going to be as easy as we thought.

After about an hour's travel, the train came abruptly to a halt. Puzzled, Yossel peered out the window. One look was enough to turn him white as a sheet.

"Russian soldiers," he whispered. "It's another check-point!"

All the passengers were ordered off the train, including our group. Our certificates were inspected carefully while Yossel and Leibel stood nearby pretending nonchalance.

After several moments, the Russian soldier looked up and eyed them with cool insolence.

"You seem to be mistaken, sirs," he said in a silky tone. "Greece is in the other direction. Come with me. I will put you on the right train, and we will send you directly to Greece. Your Greek friends must be very anxious to get home."

Poor Leibel almost fainted on the spot. What if they really sent us to Greece? If they did, it was inevitable that they would discover that our passports were false, and then who knew where we would end up? There was nothing we could do but follow orders, so Leibel and Yossel led us across the tracks and helped us board another train, heading in the "right" direction.

The train was a freight train, and Leibel stood just inside the door to give each of us a hand up. He was shaking like a leaf, cracking his knuckles constantly in his nervousness. As each of us boarded the train, he whispered in our ear, "Say *Tehillim* and pray for a miracle. If they find out we're not Greeks, they'll send us to Siberia."

The car we were boarding was little more than four walls; there was no roof, no benches and no chairs. We sat on the floor, watching with fascination as Leibel paced up and down the length of the car, mumbling to himself as we swayed along.

Actually, I wasn't feeling worried. I was getting too much pleasure out of the cool fresh air and the beautiful day to feel worried. I decided to let Leibel do the worrying for me and simply enjoy the ride.

The train came to a halt. Some of the more daring boys looked out, but there was no one in sight. There was an orchard nearby, and several of the boys jumped down and strode over to the trees that were heavy with tempting fruit.

They filled several bags with beautiful ripe plums and came back to the train to hand them out. We all pounced on the delicious fruit, marvelling at a taste that we hadn't experienced in years. The train began to move again just as we were finishing our plums, but I was too contented to care. The odd looks Sarah was giving me made me realize that my attitude was more than a little peculiar, but somehow I couldn't bring myself to care.

The sun had already set when the train finally stopped at a small Czech village. We were ordered off the train and led away by several Russian soldiers. The weather-beaten sign over the station told us we were in the village of Chopp, but that didn't leave us any wiser.

Our guards led us to a large square with a hut in one corner. The square was encircled with a tall wire fence that prevented anyone from getting out. When the soldiers locked the gates behind us, I couldn't help giving a shudder of fear. I felt my hands start to tremble. Oh, Hashem, what are they going to do with us? Here we were, surrounded by wire fences and guards again! The memory of Auschwitz was too raw in my mind, and I was really afraid. What if Leibel was right? What if they really were going to send us to Siberia? It seemed incredibly unfair that we should survive the Nazi terror only to end up in far away, frozen Siberia.

As the skies grew darker, the weather turned chillier. No one spoke; we were afraid to speak in Polish since we were masquerading as Greeks. As we rubbed our hands together in an effort to keep warm, one of the guards opened the gate, leaned in and ordered us to go into the hut for the night.

The hut had two rooms. One was brightly lit while the other was completely dark. Nobody wanted to enter the dark area, so we all crowded into the brightly lit room. There was a small table, two chairs and an iron bed. Several girls were sitting on the bed, and a few people were sitting on the floor, but most of us just stood around and worried. We were still afraid to talk, because we didn't know if we could be overheard.

We had worked up enough courage to converse in whispers when the door abruptly opened. Complete silence fell over the room as a slim, blond, highly decorated officer swaggered in. He scanned the room with bright, intelligent eyes. Then he walked forward, and of all people, he approached me!

"*Atkuda ti?*" he asked. "From where do you come?"

I bit my lip. "*Ani lo mevina,* I don't understand," I mumbled in Hebrew. It worked in Poland, I thought desperately. Maybe it will work here.

It didn't. "Oh!" His face lighted up. "*Aht medaberet Ivrit?* You speak Hebrew?"

I gulped. I knew there were Russians who spoke both Yiddish and Hebrew. No matter what language I spoke, he would surely recognize that it wasn't Greek. What should I do?

A long, agonizing moment went by before Pola Rothschild broke the frozen tableau. She stepped forward and said in a loud, clear voice, "I speak Hebrew. What would you like to know?"

The soldier started talking to her eagerly in rapid Hebrew. After a few moments, they switched to Polish. It seemed that the soldier was a Polish Jew serving in the Russian Army. He promised to take care of us, but he warned us not to talk to any of the other soldiers.

The young man seemed quite taken with Sarah, and he spent a great deal of time chatting with her. I was nervous and

239

SISTERS IN THE STORM

uneasy when I saw this; I couldn't get the behavior of those
two Russian soldiers on the train to Lodz out of my mind. I
was afraid to go near the two of them, but I kept a wary eye
on them. Fortunately, the young soldier seemed very polite
and proper.

"Do not be afraid," he reassured her. "I wouldn't harm
you. I'll protect you and your entire group."

I, too, was reassured. This Russian soldier was an honest,
compassionate man. As he left the hut, he walked on tiptoes
so he would not awaken those who had fallen asleep. I was
greatly relieved, and I drifted off to sleep, my worries forgotten.

At daybreak, our young soldier returned. He told us to
wake everyone up and get ready to leave. Once everyone had
their knapsacks slung over their shoulders, the soldier escorted us to the train station where we had gotten off the
previous evening. Then it had been deserted, but now it was
humming, with thousands of people waiting for the train.
When the train pulled into the station, it was as if the crowd
exploded. Throngs of people carrying suitcases, huge boxes
or baskets with chickens, geese or ducklings swarmed onto
the train. People were even climbing onto the roof. Looking
at the astonishing spectacle, I thought that we would never
get on board the train.

Our young soldier, however, had other ideas. Together
with another Russian in uniform, they cleared a way for us
and found us room on the train. We were all packed into one
small boxcar, but we breathed a sigh of relief when we finally
pulled out of the station.

Leibel's face was aglow, his grin stretching from ear to
ear. He kept repeating, "We're safe, we're safe! We're not
going to Siberia!" Everyone was laughing and joking in an

excess of relief. I hugged Sarah, happy that we had managed to escape the Russian regime. We were going in the right direction now; the train would take us to Vienna, and we would go on to Budapest after a day's wait in the Viennese train station. Soon we would be able to continue our trip to Eretz Yisrael!

BOOK FIVE

The
Aftermath
of the
Storm

# CHAPTER 32

■

# A Question of Directions

O N SEPTEMBER 5, 1945, WE ARRIVED IN BUDAPEST. WE were met by a delegation from Agudas Yisrael, and they put us on a trolley which took us directly to the Agudah office in the heart of Budapest. Leibel and Yossel, who knew most of the people in the Agudah, began to discuss our trip and the plans for our group's future.

The last thing we were interested in was the future; we were much more interested in a hot shower, a good meal and a place to sleep. The Agudah leaders evidently understood this, because as soon as we arrived at the office, we were taken to a large room and presented with a lavish meal. It felt wonderful to have a decent meal, and we all began to feel much better.

Soon after we finished eating, we boarded the trolleys

again and rode to the university building, where the Agudah had reserved two large halls for us. The second floor was for the girls and the third floor was for the boys. There were shower facilities, and there was a mad dash to be the first one to experience the luxury of being clean. The whole group began to take on a festive air. We were safe, we were well-fed, we were clean—what more could we ask for? Each of us received a bundle of straw and a blanket for our bedding. We arranged our bundles of straw on the floor and stretched out on our blankets, laughing and talking late into the night. Finally, we all dropped off to sleep out of sheer exhaustion.

Since the university was some distance from the Agudah offices, we had to take a trolley every time we were called together for a meeting. At the meetings, we were informed of our rights and the various options open to us. One meeting involved a discussion on whether or not to cross the border into Italy and join a group of immigrants there. Our other option was to wait in Budapest until such a group was arranged in town.

Our leaders stressed that the trip into Italy would not be an easy one. It would involve weeks of travel by night, crossing all sorts of terrain—snow-covered mountains, wide rivers and rough ground. There would be no shelter, and we would be completely dependent on our guide to get us there safely.

The boys in the group were enthusiastic about the proposal. They were still young enough at heart to believe they were capable of doing just about anything. I, on the other hand, was dismayed at the idea. As a result of the malnutrition I had suffered in the ghetto, I had edema, which caused my feet to swell terribly. The edema had nearly cost me my life when Sarah and I had been trapped in the fields of

Marishin. I was very frightened at the idea that I would have to climb mountains and walk long distances. I was glad to see that most of the other girls weren't interested in the trip to Italy. At least I wasn't the only person to disagree with the boys.

We discussed it back and forth, but we were at an impasse. The boys wanted to travel to Italy, and the girls wanted to stay in Budapest. One of the boys suggested that they could go on to Italy on their own, leaving the girls behind. Tempers were beginning to fray when two delegates from Bucharest, Sender Bergman and Itche Goldwasser, spoke up. They told us that if we didn't want to go to Italy, we would be more than welcome in Bucharest.

"There are children *streaming* into Bucharest!" said Goldwasser expansively. "There is a dire need for teachers there. Come to Bucharest, and an immigration group will be formed very quickly from all the refugees coming into the city!"

The compromise satisfied all of us. The boys shouldered their knapsacks once more and headed to Italy, and the girls boarded another train and travelled towards Romania, where we would find jobs as teachers in the city of Bucharest.

It was late Thursday night when our train pulled into Deberczen, Hungary. We were utterly exhausted, but we had no place to stay. We ended up sleeping in the station on the floor. In the morning, however, Yossel made his way into town and came back with a group of enthusiastic Jews who insisted on inviting us into their homes for *Shabbos*.

Sarah and I were placed together in a home. The three children stared at us for some time before they got over their shyness and started to play with us. I closed my eyes, remembering a home before the war that had also had three children named Binyamin, Chanka and Sarah. Out of the happy family of five, there were only two of us left. The normalcy of our hosts' home was a poignant reminder of how much we had lost.

The woman stood by the table that night, her eyes glowing as bright as the match with which she lit her *Shabbos* candles. Watching her, I had no trouble imagining she was really Mammeshe standing in her lovely green silk dress. Later in the evening, I had the same eerie feeling, when the woman's husband came home and made *Kiddush*. Even the *zemiros* they sang were the same tunes Binyamin had sung. The beauty of the *Shabbos* hammered home how much we didn't have. I made myself a solemn promise that night that someday I, too, would have a normal, happy home where *Shabbos* and *Yom Tov* would be kept as they had been in my parents' home.

After a delicious *Shabbos seudah*, our hostess escorted us into a room where we would sleep. She treated us like princesses, providing us with feather quilts and pillows so that we would sleep comfortably. I hadn't seen a feather pillow since the pre-war years!

After a delightful night's sleep, we were given homemade cake and milk for our breakfast before *davening*. We spent the entire *Shabbos* in their home, basking in the warmth of a normal religious family. Yes, it hurt to see their life and remember that I had lost what they took for granted, but it was wonderful to share in it nevertheless.

We thanked our hosts, then returned to the station to join the rest of the group. We boarded the train and resumed our journey. We crossed the border into Romania, and we soon arrived in Bucharest.

The Agudah in Bucharest welcomed us warmly, providing us with all our needs. However, we were dismayed to discover that the need for teachers in Bucharest had been grossly exaggerated. There were only fifty or sixty students, and the three women working in the school had years of experience. We, on the other hand, were a bunch of girls who had received little education since the war broke up the *shiurim* we had attended in Bnos. Disappointed, we had to find some other jobs with which to keep ourselves occupied while waiting for the chance to immigrate to Eretz Yisrael.

We ended up staying in Bucharest for a little more than a year. In general, the year was a pleasant one, even though there were some uncomfortable times and moments of disillusionment. Still, these setbacks were minor compared to the great deal of emotional and intellectual bounty we were given during our stay.

I gained a great deal for myself during my year in Bucharest. I studied Hebrew with Pola Rothschild, the girl who had spoken up in the little hut in Russia. Pola Weltfried, who had offered me half her roll on the initial part of our journey, joined me in taking a designing and dressmaking course that came in handy when we got jobs in a textile factory office. I was able to gain a great deal of learning, as well, as the teachers of the school offered to give *shiurim* to the older refugees in the evenings.

Besides intellectual advantage, I had the wonderful opportunity to help others during my stay in Bucharest. Together with Pola Weltfried, I quit my well-paying job in the textile factory office to work as a volunteer secretary in the Agudah office.

Pola and I were extremely surprised when Shmelke Dachner came to us and offered us the job. He explained that our fluency in the Yiddish language and our ability to write and type in Yiddish were exactly what was needed. Our job would be to interview the children arriving in Bucharest and get an account of their experiences during the war. Dachner warned us that there was no salary for the job, but he pointed out that we would find it extremely rewarding. He offered to give us some time to think it over, but we assured him that it was unnecessary. The two of us started our new job the next day.

On our first day on the job, most of the children were refugees from Russia who had been left in gentile homes or monasteries during the war. Their parents had never returned for them, and they were coming to Bucharest on their own in search of shelter and a home.

Pola and I worked together on each child. One of us would talk to the child, trying to draw him out and get him to speak. Meanwhile, the other one would sit unobtrusively in a corner and jot down any information the child provided. Once we had gotten all the information we possibly could, we escorted the child back outside and filed the information.

The job was anything but easy. Sometimes we dealt with children who were only six or seven years old. They were unable to tell us their parents' names or the name of the city in which they were born. We often had to cross-check our information, recalling and questioning an older child who had been in the same monastery or convent. Using information provided by these older children, we were often able to piece together the history of the little ones whose parents were little more than a vague memory. The pictures attached to each file were also very helpful, as other children often recognized a picture of a younger brother or sister.

Pola and I spent hours researching the convents and monasteries where children had been kept. Once we knew the background, we were able to ask the leading questions that would help us determine who these children were and if they had any relatives that could help them.

I really enjoyed my job. Although it hurt me to hear horror story after horror story, it gave me great satisfaction to know that I was helping homeless children find a place to live. Every child with a happy ending was an additional setback to the Nazis' intention to wipe out the Jewish race.

# CHAPTER 33

A Dreadful Disappointment

S ATISFYING JOB NOTWITHSTANDING, I HAD NO INTEN-
tion of remaining in Bucharest. My goal was to reach
Eretz Yisrael, and I waited impatiently for the chance
to leave.

In the meantime, my friend Pola Weltfried got engaged to
a boy whose parents lived in Bucharest. They also planned to
go to Eretz Yisrael, but they intended to do it legally. I was
delighted for her, even though I was a little sad that now we
would have to go our separate ways. I determined to use the
knowledge I had gained in dressmaking to sew her a few skirts
and blouses as a wedding gift.

I wondered if I would still be in Bucharest for the
wedding. Half of me longed to be at Pola's *chasunah*, but the
other half of me wanted to leave Romania as soon as possible.

It would be pointless to stay in Bucharest for the wedding if an opportunity to go to Eretz Yisrael would arise. In the end, an order came to pack and make ourselves ready. There was a ship waiting for us in the seaport of Constanca. We were on our way!

I bid tearful good-byes to Pola. I was sorry she wasn't coming with us. I left her gift in her room along with a letter of farewell before I went to join the transport.

After a sleepless night spent imagining life in Eretz Yisrael, our transport left Bucharest at the crack of dawn. We travelled down to the seaport and arrived there at midday.

The noise in the port was deafening. Thousands of people were waiting impatiently to get on the ship *Smyrna*, which was anchored at the dock. I was glad that we had our certificates, naming us as passengers; there were many more people milling around on the dock than there were places on board the ship.

Hours passed, but no one was allowed to board the ship. We sat down on the chilly asphalt ground as the day slowly waned. Throughout that long, cold night, we sat and waited for the chance to get on board. It's all worth it, I kept telling myself. It's all worth it as long as we get to go to Eretz Yisrael.

At daybreak, our leaders roused us and ordered us into line. Eagerly, we lined up and waited for our names to be called to board the ship. Name after name was called, and I watched anxiously as the ship slowly filled with passengers. When were they going to call us?

Suddenly, I gave a start. They had just called the name of one of the girls in our group! But when she tried to step forward, the members of another group held her back. I watched with disbelief as another woman calmly walked forward to take her place. What was going on?

SISTERS IN THE STORM

Our seats were being taken, I realized with horror. Our seats had been sold to other people. We were victims of the black market, and all our seats were gone!

Our Agudah leaders ran over to the ship authorities and began a heated argument. We didn't know what was going on, but we anxiously strained our ears to overhear what was happening. They came walking back, shaking their heads and looking upset. I overheard one of them say, "Only two certificates left."

Two certificates for one hundred people? Two people were going to be chosen to board the ship? An undercurrent of excitement and anxiety ran through the group. Who would be the two lucky girls that would get a chance to go to Eretz Yisrael?

Finally, one of the leaders beckoned to Sarah. She hesitantly stepped forward. He told Regina Braun to come with him as well, and the three of them stepped aside to talk.

"We managed to bribe the ship authorities," he said heavily. "They only gave us two certificates. Regina, I want you to take one of them. You're not well, and we need to get you to Eretz Yisrael as soon as possible. And you, Sarah, you're the youngest in our group. You deserve the chance to start a normal life. I'm giving the other certificate to you."

Regina accepted immediately, but Sarah refused to take the certificate. She argued that she was no more deserving than anyone else, and she didn't want to be the cause of jealousy and animosity among the other girls. I was furious with her when I found out what she had done. After waiting for months, how could she turn down the opportunity?

By the time I found out what Sarah had done, it was too late. Her ticket had already been given to an older woman. The screaming and crying rent the air. We were all utterly furious at the way we had been deceived. How could they do this to us? Had they no shame?

We found out later that the Zionists had been granted a number of certificates by Queen Victoria on the condition that only young people were sent to Palestine. Unfortunately, there were some Jewish officials who conspired to fill their pockets at our expense. Our group had been allowed into port to maintain the illusion that young people were being sent, but once protocol had been satisfied, they had no compunction in giving our seats to someone else. We had run into a similar problem in Bucharest, when we discovered that the money the Polish government provided for Polish refu- gees was not being distributed to us. In the wake of the war, a great deal of *mentchlachkeit* and decency had gone out the window. It was our misfortune to fall victim to the pettiness and greed of those few leaders who fell prey to the tempta- tions of corruption. Still, even now, I can't condemn them completely. Much as they caused us suffering, the amount of good they did for us far outweighed the bad.

None of us was aware of this at the time. All we knew was that the gangway had been removed and there was no way to get on board the *Smyrna*. We were enraged and completely helpless to do anything about it.

The only thing connecting the ship to land was the narrow board balanced from an upper porthole, used to roll cargo on board the ship. I looked at the barrels and crates with envy. Why couldn't I go on board instead of them?

Suddenly, I caught my breath. There was a lull in the hauling, and none of the sailors was near the board. Elka Hapner, one of our girls, was climbing up the board to the ship! I watched her in terror. How could she climb up so high? If she fell, it would be like falling out of a third-story window in a building. The entire board vibrated violently with every move she made, but she stubbornly kept going. I breathed a sigh of relief when I saw her make it onto the ship. She quickly slipped through the porthole and mingled with the other passengers.

Two others followed her lead. Kozak, the young man who had given me a place to sleep in Lodz, was one of them. They, too, mingled with the passengers and managed to escape notice. I sighed again, only now my relief was tinged with envy. Elka, Kozak and Devora Borenstien were on board. They would be going to Eretz Yisrael! Why couldn't I go, too?

Just before sundown, the ship lifted anchor and sailed away. A moan rose from the dock, a collective groan of dismay from all those that were still standing there. We looked with longing after the *Smyrna*. It grew smaller and smaller as it sailed away, finally vanishing over the horizon. Our group was silent as we shouldered our knapsacks and returned to Bucharest, broken and depressed.

# CHAPTER 34

---
■
---

# The Real Thing

N ONE OF US WAS VERY HAPPY TO BE BACK. HOWEVER, *Pesach* was just around the corner, and there was a lot to be done. We couldn't move back into the apartment where we had stayed before, so we found a new apartment a few blocks away from the Agudah offices. We had no kitchen, so we had to go to the Agudah for meals.

The new apartment was awful. We were utterly plagued by bedbugs! Sarah used to joke that we moved in *Erev Pesach* and we were getting a taste of what the Egyptians suffered during the plague of lice. All joking aside, it reached the point where we couldn't even lie down to sleep! Even when we stood in the middle of the brightly lit room, as far away from the beds as possible, the bedbugs still swarmed out to attack us.

Finally, out of desperation, we decided to burn the mattresses, figuring that the bedbugs' nests were in them. We dragged the mattresses into the back yard and set fire to them. We laughed as we watched the bedbugs frantically scurrying out of their hiding places, swarming through the wooden fence into the yard next door. We were happy to be rid of them.

The highlight of our stay in that apartment came later that night. The house next door was a fancy nightclub, and the singing and dancing often kept us awake long into the night. That evening, while our mattresses were still smoldering in the yard, we heard terrible screams and shouts coming from the nightclub. Sarah and I rushed outside to find out what was happening. The nightclub owner was literally dancing with frustration. His tables, dishes and floors were swarming with bedbugs! He cursed right and left as he was forced to close the nightclub.

Sarah and I were laughing so hard that we retreated into our apartment, hoping the owner wouldn't realize that it was our fault he was being attacked by bedbugs. We hadn't done it on purpose, but we later agreed that there wasn't another Romanian who deserved it more than that nightclub owner. At any rate, it took him over a week before he managed to fumigate the place and open for business again.

We spent an endless summer in Bucharest, waiting impatiently in the heat for another call to leave. Pola's in-laws often invited Sarah and me to come to their home for *Shabbos*. It was wonderful to see Pola so happy and glowing with her future husband at her side! Often, those pleasant *Shabbosim* spent with Pola seemed to be the only bright spots in our stay in Bucharest. We were frustrated by our trip to Constanca, and we were wary of another transport that might end in the same miserable fashion. Still, the two of us agreed that it was better to risk disappointment than not to have the chance to go to Eretz Yisrael at all.

Towards the end of the summer, rumors began to circulate that there was going to be another attempt to organize an immigration group. Our enthusiasm was marred by the bad taste that still lingered in our mouths from the disappointing trip to Constanca. The rumors persisted longer than usual, and we began to wonder if maybe it was actually true.

Then, on a *Motzei Shabbos* right before the month of *Elul,* the word passed quietly from ear to ear. Get ready! We're leaving! The whole thing was done in secrecy. We weren't even told where we were going.

We left our rooms at midnight. We marched several miles in complete darkness and silence. At one point, we were met by several wagons. We were told to jump onto the wagons. Covering ourselves with blankets, we huddled in the back of the wagons as they rolled quietly into the village of Arad.

In Arad, we got off the wagons and waited in subdued silence. Suddenly, we heard the low growling sound of trucks driving in low gear coming towards us. The trucks rolled to a stop several feet away, and we were led in that direction. Several people that were waiting for us helped us board the trucks. As we left the village, we coasted in neutral whenever possible to minimize the noise. The trucks rolled on and on as we dozed in the warm darkness.

At about noontime on the following day, we reached the city of Belgrade. The trucks stopped at the coast, and we boarded the small boat that was waiting for us.

By this time, we had grown confident that this trip was the real thing. Too much had happened already; we felt assured that we wouldn't end up back in Bucharest again. We began to enjoy ourselves, basking in the warmth of the sun and enjoying our pleasant boat ride. After several hours, the boat sailed into port. We disembarked in the city of Zagreb, Yugoslavia.

# CHAPTER 35

■

# Marking Time in Zagreb

W E ARRIVED IN ZAGREB JUST BEFORE *ROSH HASHANAH*. It was a delightful little town, a far cry from the dreary industrial pollution of Lodz. I was enchanted by the magnificent background of the snow-covered mountains, which only served to emphasize the warm weather down in Zagreb itself. However, much as I wanted to wander through the streets of thatched cottages and shady trees, I knew that we were illegals, refugees trying to make it to Eretz Yisrael. Zagreb was only another step along the way. It was crucial that we remained unseen by the Yugoslavian authorities.

Our group was led to an abandoned, half-finished factory building at the end of town, situated at the foot of the mountains. The building, four stories high, was stark and dreary, looking for all the world like a bunch of bricks piled up on top of each other. There were several gaps in the walls, obviously meant to be windows and doors, but they had never been completed. The staircases were left unfinished; there were steep ramps in place, but the steps and rails had never been constructed. It was the perfect haven for us, since nobody in their right mind would want to go there.

As soon as we filed into the building, our leaders began to organize us. The building was packed, and the echoes seemed to bounce back at us from all sides. Every group of illegal refugees in Zagreb was there, groups from Poland as well as other countries. The Agudah was only one group; there was also a group organized by Beitar and several others.

Since the Agudah group was relatively small, we were put on the third floor together with the members of another group. Sarah and I exchanged glances. I hoped that the common bond of reaching Eretz Yisrael would continue to neutralize any arguments or disagreements. We would be living in very close quarters with people of very different convictions.

Suddenly, it dawned on me that we would have to get up to the third floor. The absence of any staircase made the whole idea seem a little ridiculous, and I wondered how they expected us to get up there. I looked at the steep ramps. Surely they didn't expect us to *climb* those things, did they?

They did. "You'll have to race up and down the slopes," announced our leader. "Don't walk or try to climb slowly. It's much too dangerous. Don't stop in the middle of the flight, and don't go up with another person. Go up and down the slopes one at a time, and you should be all right."

I noticed that he said "should," not "will." Still, everyone else seemed willing to do it, so I didn't seem to have any choice. One of the boys in my group offered to take up my knapsack for me, making it easier for me to race up the slopes without any weight holding me down. I managed the race up the slopes, relieved to get up to the third floor in one piece.

I made a beeline for one of the gaps in the wall. It was supposed to be a window, but there was no glass separating me from the crisp, cool air as I leaned out. The view was absolutely gorgeous! The mountains looked like a painting, snow-covered hills against a backdrop of deep blue sky. For a moment, I almost forgot that I was an illegal refugee, running the risk of being arrested at any moment. Then I turned away from the mountains to face what was going on around me, and I was brought back to reality in a hurry.

The state of affairs inside the building seemed even worse by contrast to the lovely outdoors. Our new living quarters consisted of a bare cement floor and nothing else. We had no closets, no shelves and no beds. There was a huge stack of hay piled haphazardly along the east wall, with several musty blankets heaped alongside the hay. At first, I thought that the huge building had originally been a barn, but then I realized that the hay and blankets were going to be our beds. It was the only luxury of living we were going to have for the next two months.

When we went to sleep at night, the fresh air coming in from the open "windows" turned icy cold. Our leaders tried to improvise by covering the windows with the cardboard from several cartons they had dug up from somewhere. The result was that the wind blew in with a little less violence, but the room was much darker and it was difficult to see. The solution lasted for only a few weeks before the constant dampness rotted the cardboard to pieces. We had to come up with another way to keep warm.

Sarah and I shared our hay and blankets with three other girls. Each of us was issued one blanket, so we used one as a sheet to spread over the hay and piled the other four on top of us. Huddled together underneath the blankets, we tried to warm each other, but it was useless. We shivered all night, and we often woke up in the morning to find a fine dusting of snow covering our blankets.

We had absolutely no privacy. The entire third floor was one vast room, so we all slept along the walls without any separations. The few couples among us managed to build "separate" sleeping quarters by piling up several bricks they had collected in the yard. The boys in the Agudah groups slept as far away as possible from the girls at the other end of the room. We all dressed and undressed underneath our blankets, and if someone wanted to change during the day, two of the girls would hold a blanket in front of her to act as a curtain. We all made the best of it, doing what we could to make life a little easier.

When we woke up each morning, our teeth were chattering so hard it was almost impossible to speak. Racing down three flights of "stairs," however, was enough to warm us up. The washroom, laundry room, shower and kitchen were on the main floor. Nothing worked very well; I learned first-hand about the joys of taking an ice-cold shower in freezing weather. Hot water, even for the kitchen, was non-existent.

Familiarity with the steep ramps didn't lessen their danger. Once, when we were racing down the slopes, another girl crashed into Sarah and sent her tumbling down to the next floor. The girl rushed to Sarah's side and burst into tears, saying over and over how sorry she was for hurting her. Poor Sarah, who had taken the brunt of the fall on her back, still has trouble with her spine today.

The Agudah boys *davened* with a *minyan* three times a day and had several learning sessions as well. We girls didn't have any organized *davening* except for *Shabbos,* and there were no classes for us at all. If one of us wanted to learn, she had to do it on her own.

There wasn't really anything to do in Zagreb. We spent as much time outside of the building as possible, but the cold weather often drove us indoors for shelter. One boy in my Agudah group used to tell stories to an eager crowd of listeners, and even the non-religious refugees would listen spellbound. However, after several weeks, the boy stopped his nightly storytelling. We were left to our own devices to find something to do.

Perhaps the reason there was nothing to occupy our time was that our leaders expected to be given the order to depart at any given moment. They certainly didn't expect us to remain in Zagreb for over two months! Because of all the uncertainties, we had no program of activities, learning or otherwise, with which to occupy our time. We wandered up and down the halls, talking about the past and trying to envision the future. The few books that had been brought along were always in great demand, but there were hardly enough to go around.

I felt dissatisfied with doing nothing. I wanted to learn something, do something, so I would feel like I wasn't wasting my time! In the end, I found one worthwhile project. There was an older man named Harlik, whose daughter had been with me in Romania. He was all alone, and nobody seemed to care about him. I offered to do the old man's laundry for him; he seemed happier about having somebody who was interested in him than about the prospect of getting his laundry done. I washed his laundry for the entire two months we were in Zagreb, feeling better about having something to do. In fact, I ended up making a pair of pajamas for him out of an old tent.

Our self-imposed confinement became too much for me. I felt as if I was suffocating in the dreary building. One evening, I sneaked out of the building together with two of my friends. We knew we were supposed to remain in the area and avoid contact with the Yugoslavians, but I needed to get into town and see for myself that I wasn't in a prison. I wanted to know that there was still laughter and joking in the world, not just shivering under blankets while lying on bales of hay.

We were not the first ones to disobey the order to stay out of the city. We had heard that there was a cafeteria on the outskirts of town which other Agudah members had visited, and we made the cafeteria our destination.

We walked into the cafeteria. It was clean, bright and noisy. We walked up to the counter and ordered black coffee, the only thing we knew would be kosher. The coffee soon arrived, thick, black, aromatic coffee in a tiny cup. I inhaled deeply, enjoying the delicious smell of that coffee. I had never tasted coffee like that in my life, and I savored every sip with great enjoyment.

We listened to the conversations going on around us. The *goyim* were speaking an unknown Slavic language, but it was similar enough to Polish for me to understand what they were saying. Two girls were seated at the table next to us, talking in low voices. They looked Jewish to me, and I wanted to speak to them and ask them questions; but then I remembered that we had to remain "invisible" and refrain from contact with anyone that was not part of our group. With regret, we finished drinking our extraordinary coffee and slowly made our way back to our headquarters, the drab brick building at the foot of the mountains.

One evening, while I was walking outside in the courtyard with Sarah, we heard a sudden commotion from inside the building. We rushed inside to find the whole place in an uproar. The order had come: Start packing immediately! We have to leave right away!

I was ecstatic at the idea of finally leaving Zagreb. Much as I enjoyed the lovely scenery, I was chafing to continue on our journey. Thrilled that we were finally on the move, I raced upstairs to get my few things packed into my knapsack. In my haste and excitement, I found myself dropping two items for every one that I packed. Bending down to pick something up, I managed to trip on the strap of my knapsack and went sprawling on the ground.

I sat down for a moment, telling myself firmly that I had to get myself organized. Forcing myself to work calmly and slowly, I finished my packing. I was just tightening the straps when the lights went out.

The room, which had been alive with the sound of hundreds of chattering people, fell instantly silent. Into the stillness came the voice of our leader, ordering us to quietly file toward the exit and go down to the main floor of the building.

Without a sound, we all headed toward the slopes. When my turn arrived to dash downstairs, someone took my knapsack and slid it down the slope ahead of me. I joined the crowd in the main hall, pausing only to scoop up my knapsack and sling it over my back. Everyone was filing quietly outdoors in their small groups. I quickly joined my own Agudah group and followed them outside, where our guide was waiting for us.

Each group had its own guide. As soon as our group was

all together, the guide gestured for us to follow and started walking rapidly away from the building. The factory building was soon left far behind.

Most of us exchanged nervous glances as we left the dubious protection of the building where we had lived for the last two months. Sarah, who had been one of the last girls to come outside, slipped her hand into mine and squeezed tightly. I gave her a grin of encouragement as we slipped into the dark, moonless night, comfortably unseen by unfriendly eyes. We were on our way!

# CHAPTER 36

■

# The Sea Voyage Begins

WE HAD BEEN WALKING FOR OVER AN HOUR, HEARING nothing but the chirping of crickets and the occasional scream of an owl. Now I became conscious of a low rumbling noise. It gradually dawned on me that it was the sound of idling engines. With rising excitement, I tapped on Sarah's shoulder, pointing first to my ear and then ahead of us. She cocked her head, listening for a moment, then smiled and nodded, indicating that she heard it, too. We began to walk faster, eager to reach the trucks that we instinctively knew were waiting for us.

Minutes later, we were ordered to halt. Straining my eyes in the darkness, I made out the shapes of several trucks waiting for us a few yards away. We clambered onto the trucks, which were open to the clear night sky. Our leader climbed onto the truck, fastening the tailgate behind him to ensure that nobody accidentally tumbled out. He waved to the driver, who was standing patiently by the door of the cab. The driver nodded, climbed into the cab of the truck and shifted into gear. I hung over the tailgate, watching the ground slide away as we slowly began our climb through the mountains.

Our ride was short but fascinating. After a slow, cautious beginning, our truck picked up speed and moved rapidly through the mountains. It was not long before we began to descend into a valley, and I soon caught the sharp, wild smell of the sea. I grew more and more excited as the ocean scents grew stronger. I knew we were approaching our destination. It seemed too good to be true!

The trucks came to a halt on a quiet seashore, and we all scrambled down. By this point, we already knew what to do without being told, and it only took a few minutes before we were all lined up in our groups and patiently waiting for our next orders. Craning my neck, I saw a light twinkling far out to sea. Perhaps that's our ship, I thought excitedly. Maybe that's the ship that will take us to Eretz Yisrael!

A half hour passed. Suddenly, there was a dark shape gliding quietly toward the shore where we were standing. Then there was another, and another, and another.

The small dinghies pulled into shore with silent precision. The lines moved quickly forward as ten people climbed into each boat. The moment a boat was full, it would swiftly turn and head back for that tantalizing light in the distance.

When my turn came, an outstretched hand grabbed my wrist and pulled me onto the little boat. It was too dark to see the man's face as he motioned to me that I should not say a word. I barely had time to settle myself onto the hard wooden bench before our boat was filled to capacity. We quickly headed away from shore towards the flickering light that beckoned so eagerly. It seemed to take only seconds before a huge ship loomed before us. The man who had helped me into the boat guided us expertly towards the side of the ship, where a rope ladder was waiting for us to climb aboard.

Although some people enjoyed the adventure of clambering up the ladder, there were many of us who had a great deal of trouble. The ladder was made of a thick rope that swayed back and forth in the waves, making it difficult to keep one's balance. One boy named David was unfortunate enough to have his glasses slip off his nose and tumble into the sea. I knew that he was almost blind without them. Those of us still waiting in the small boat tried to find them in the water, but the pair of glasses sank quickly. Poor David was going to be half-blind for the rest of the journey.

When it was my turn to board the ship, I welcomed the darkness of the night that did not let me see the waves underneath me as I climbed laboriously up the ladder. Someone was supporting my knapsack from below, taking some of the weight off my shoulders. As I neared the top of the ladder, a welcome hand reached down and helped me up the last few rungs of wet, slippery rope. Someone grabbed me by the waist and swung me down to the deck. I felt the wooden boards of the deck, scarcely daring to believe that I was actually on board. It was real, it was really true!

Someone touched my arm. I turned my head and saw a girl standing there, her eyes gleaming in the darkness.

"Welcome to the *Knesset Yisrael*," she said softly. "We're all going home."

The long procession of small boats transporting refugees from the shore to the ship lasted throughout the night. Too overwhelmed to think coherently, I merely sat cross-legged on the dock and watched the people climbing on board.

David, who had lost his glasses when he was climbing up the rope ladder, was sitting on the deck a few feet away from me, a look of bewilderment on his face. Suddenly, a girl walked up to him and handed him her own glasses.

"Fraulein Landau!" he stammered. "I-I can't take your glasses! You need them for yourself."

"Oh, no," she said with a smile. "My eyes aren't that bad. I just feel a little uncomfortable without them, that's all. Isn't that right, Chanka?" She turned towards me and gave a little shrug.

I was more impressed than I could say. *Baruch Hashem,* I didn't have to worry about my eyesight, but I didn't find it difficult to imagine what it would be like to see the entire world as a blur. Fraulein Landau's gift was generosity itself.

I was distracted by a sudden creaking that seemed to shudder through the entire ship. Everyone jumped up and ran to the rails to watch as the anchor was ponderously raised. Everyone was on board the ship! The *Knesset Yisrael* was on its way to Eretz Yisrael!

We didn't let anything dampen our spirits, not even the fact that our lovely ship was little more than a scow. It wasn't even meant for transporting passengers; it was an old, dilapidated cargo ship that was much too small for the 4,500 refugees crowded on board. But none of that mattered. So there weren't enough sleeping quarters? Who cared if there was insufficient sanitation facilities? As the *Knesset Yisrael* sailed further away from Yugoslavia, we all simultaneously burst into song, singing *"Leshanah habaah b'Yerushalayim"* at the top of our lungs. There were several little circles of dancers all over the ship, and feelings were running sky high.

We felt like nothing could stop us now!

When the levels of euphoria had dimmed to somewhat more manageable levels, one of the leaders mounted a wooden box to address us. He spoke with fervor and enthusiasm, painting a beautiful picture of the wonderful life waiting for us in Eretz Yisrael, despite the hazards we would have to overcome along the way. Most of us, however, chose to ignore the dangers. Yes, it was true that our ship was barely seaworthy. Granted, we had a low supply of food and water. We also were aware that the British were scouring the seas for illegals trying to reach Eretz Yisrael. But who cared? The knowledge that we were finally out of Europe was more than enough for now.

The day passed in a general state of cheerfulness. Skimpy rations of food and water were handed out and quickly consumed. Laughter, singing and lighthearted conversation filled the air. Everyone was riding on a wave of happiness; only the leaders seemed nervous. They were all too well aware that the British were lurking out there, waiting to pounce on us if they could find us. We, on the other hand, were too confident to think of England and the dangers of being captured. After all, we had gotten this far. Surely we would manage to get to Eretz Yisrael safely! As I climbed onto my "bed" that night—it was little more than a plank, and the next plank over my head was so low that I had to crawl to get there—I felt content and optimistic, thinking that the entire trip would be as enjoyable as the first day.

I woke up the next morning in a very different state of mind. I was miserably, horribly seasick. Most people tumbled off their planks and made their way back up to the deck, where the singing and dancing resumed as if they had never stopped in the first place. I just curled up in a ball and wished

273

that the ship would stop rocking. The mere idea of food was enough to make me sick. I was feverish and filthy. I longed for a clean bed and medicine, but such things were nonexistent on the ship. There was nothing I could do to help myself except moan softly and try to shut out the world.

By the fourth day, I was feeling well enough to make my shaky way up to the deck. Leaning on the rail, feeling the cool breeze on my face, I began to regain some of the ebullient confidence of the first day. I spent several hours just standing by the rail and marvelling at the beauty of the ocean.

Our leaders, however, were growing more and more apprehensive. They were weighing their options, trying to decide whether they should risk going on or if it would be wiser to turn back. The weather was perfect—too perfect, since clear skies meant the British would have an easier time finding us. The final decision was to make use of a "holding pattern," circling over the same spot and sailing back and forth over and over again, until the leaders felt it was a good time to risk the run across the sea towards Eretz Yisrael.

A week passed, a week full of growing uncertainties. No one was dancing or singing anymore. We were running low on food and water, and everyone felt dirty and depressed. The ship seemed filthier than ever, and we all knew that we weren't really getting anywhere. People started getting sick, and there was nothing anybody could do to help them.

I, too, was feeling ill. I felt restless and uncomfortable every time I tried to lie down on my plank, and I couldn't force myself to eat anything. In the end, I crawled off my plank, went up the deck and found myself a grimy corner in which to curl up. I closed my eyes, stretched out on the floor and stayed there for days. People stepped over me; some of them actually stepped on top of me. I remember thinking at one point that it would be much simpler if I just died, but something inside me insisted that I must defy the Nazis by living long enough to step foot on the shores of Eretz Yisrael. So I continued to live in misery, clinging to my dreams as my only lifeline.

Another week dragged by. Suddenly, the situation changed. We were advised that confrontation with the British was inevitable. Those of us looking over the rails began to point out the tiny specks on the horizon. There was no doubt in our minds that those tiny specks were British ships. Cans were distributed to each of us together with some type of explosive material, and we were instructed in the art of homemade grenades. Our leaders wanted to ensure that we would be able to defend ourselves when the British came.

# CHAPTER 37

———————■———————

## Encounters with the British

T
HREE DAYS AFTER THE FIRST BRITISH SHIP WAS
sighted, a huge military ship slipped over the
horizon and headed straight towards us. Two
other ships followed right after her, gleaming with all the spit
and polish of the distinctive British sense of order. The
British ships gracefully slipped around us, keeping us surrounded while maintaining their distance. We all watched
nervously from the deck, tight-lipped at the sight of our
enemies. No one spoke as we kept a grim eye on the three
ships sailing around us like hungry metal sharks. Two days
passed in an uneasy vigil as the three enemy ships did nothing
but watch as we sailed on.

On the third day, the British began an attempt to communicate. They signalled to us in Morse code, demanding that

we surrender our ship and transfer all passengers to their vessels. Our leaders ignored them for a long time before finally replying in the negative. Despite our hunger and exhaustion, we put on a brave front and cheered our leader's refusal. None of us had the slightest intention of giving in to the British.

Next, the British asked if we needed any medical assistance. Did we have any ill people or any pregnant women on board ship? Did we need some help or assistance in any other way?

No, our leaders told them. We don't need your help, and we certainly don't want it. We just want you to leave us alone and go away.

The truth was, of course, that we needed medical attention very badly. We had been on starvation rations for over a week, and many of us were very sick. In addition, there were two women well into their ninth month of pregnancy. Still, we were determined to present a united front towards the British, and no one said a word.

The exchange lasted a full day and well into the night. The next morning, we were astonished to see the sun rise over a sea that was apparently deserted! Where had the British ships gone? Had they given up? Were they going to leave us alone? Maybe it had all been a test and our refusal to take anything meant they would let us sail on in peace. Excited, optimistic comments buzzed back and forth. We were still hungry, thirsty and sick, but a renewed feeling of confidence filled the air.

Our cheerfulness didn't last very long. It was still well before noon when the dreaded specks appeared over the horizon. We were dismayed to see an entire contingent of British ships bearing down on us. We were just a handful of

277

refugees on an old dilapidated cargo ship. Why did England find it necessary to subdue us with such a huge display of might?

This time, the ships quickly bridged the distance between us, coming ominously close. The flagship was near enough for the captain to address us with a megaphone. Once again, he demanded that we surrender our ship. He offered us food, drink and medical help if we would surrender quietly. When we refused, the British ships settled more closely around us. We were forced to a standstill, under siege in the middle of the sea.

For the next several days, we were bombarded by announcements from the British ships, demanding our surrender. They grew more and more persistent; it wasn't long before they were threatening to fire on us if we didn't give in. Most of us found it difficult to believe our ears. These were the Allies, the soldiers that had liberated us from the death camps?

Finally, our leaders came on deck and shouted back that we would never surrender. The British answer was swift and violent. One of the ships came surging forward and crashed directly into us!

The impact was awful. It felt as if the entire ship was going to shudder apart. Those of us who were still below deck came rushing up to see the horrible and frightening sight of the British soldiers, lining the decks of their ships armed with rifles.

For a second, nobody knew what to do. We knew that England didn't want us in Eretz Yisrael, but would they actually shoot? They had already crashed into us. What was next?

Suddenly, one boy began to sing. The tune was quickly

picked up, and in moments, the bewildered British were faced with a shipful of young people, singing on the top of their lungs. It was the last thing they had expected. Resistance, yes, but singing?

For a moment, the soldiers remained immobilized. Then, with a shout, they all jerked their rifles skyward and let off a volley of shots into the air. The noise was terrifying, but most of us bent down to scoop up our homemade grenades, the sardine cans filled with explosive chemicals. Then we were staring straight down the barrels of the English guns as they opened fire at us.

Most of us dived to the deck. I heard shouts of terror and screams of pain as people were hit. One *chassidishe* boy, whose *peyos* and black hat reminded me of the happier times before the war, was standing right next to me. He was the son of the Nadvorner Rebbe, and he was going to join his uncle in Eretz Yisrael; I watched with horror as he fell dead at my feet.

I couldn't take my eyes off the pool of blood that was slowly forming underneath him. Hashem, how could we come so far only to be killed by those that had rescued us from the Germans?

Our sardine cans were no match for guns. Our "grenades" clattered to the deck, and we stood there in numbed silence as the British threw a plank over the rails to form a bridge to the *Knesset Yisrael*. They ordered us all to transfer to their ship, but no one moved.

Several British officers with exasperated looks on their faces went below deck to discuss what to do with us. We stared back at the British soldiers with hollow eyes. Did they feel guilty, I wondered, for causing suffering to those that had suffered so much already?

279

When the officers came back, they asked us if we were ready to receive some water and food. We refused, although we were in desperate need of assistance; besides the boy who had been killed, several other men had been wounded, and the two women in advanced months of pregnancy were in very serious condition. Nevertheless, all of us remained stubbornly silent.

In the end, they simply fastened a chain to the bow of our ship and towed us behind them. We moved swiftly through the water, sailing faster than we had when we were under our own power. No one spoke. We just stood on the deck, silently watching as we journeyed in the right direction, but in the wrong hands.

Towards sundown, we sighted land ahead. We all grew tremendously excited. Was it really Eretz Yisrael? Had we actually come to our final, long awaited destination? As we came closer to the land, we saw lights twinkling at us from a mountaintop.

"That's Mount Carmel," one girl whispered with awe. "Eliyahu Hanavi stood there!"

Mount Carmel, in Haifa! We were there, we had arrived, we were in Eretz Yisrael! The entire group burst out in song once again. Several of us had tears of joy streaming down our cheeks. We had finally arrived, but would they let us disembark?

There was wild speculation going on all over the ship. Someone suggested that our refusal of all assistance would enable us to enter Eretz Yisrael. Another person said that since the British had caused us casualties, they would be forced to let us disembark. It didn't take long, however, before we realized that the British had no intention of letting us go. The tears of joy turned into tears of bitter pain. It was heartbreaking to know we were so close to our goal and yet still unable to reach it.

British officers jumped onto the deck of the *Knesset Yisrael*, making us officially prisoners. How ironic, I thought bitterly. We suffered under the Nazi regime for over five years, and now we're the prisoners of the people who freed us!

The body of the dead boy was delivered to an Israeli representative, along with the two pregnant women and three men suffering from heart problems. The rest of us were ordered to transfer to the British ship. This time, we had no choice.

With trembling knees, I climbed the narrow iron ladder leading to the enemy ship. A soldier helped me up the steps. Another gave me a hand as I climbed onto the deck. They were all so polite to us, but I felt anger and fury at these men who had snatched the opportunity of going to Eretz Yisrael away from us.

For all that the British ship was clean and airy, it still felt like a prison. Yes, it was much more comfortable than the *Knesset Yisrael*, but it was going in the wrong direction! Where were they going to take us now? Would we ever make it to Eretz Yisrael?

The soldiers moved among us, distributing biscuits and encouraging us to eat. Our leaders told us that we were starting a hunger strike, and nobody was to eat anything. I was tired and dispirited. What was the point of a hunger strike? For that matter, what was the point of doing anything at all?

The British ship moved smoothly through the waters, taking us further and further away from Eretz Yisrael with every passing second. After a short journey, we arrived at the

281

island of Cyprus. It was after midnight, and the entire world seemed peaceful and quiet, but I was bitterly aware that it would be a long time before I could step foot on the hallowed soil of Eretz Yisrael.

# CHAPTER 38

■

# Settling In

THOUSANDS OF JEWS SPENT MONTHS IN THE CAMPS OF Cyprus, Jews that had come through the crucible of Europe. I remember how frightening it was for me; when we were led inside the barbed wire fences, and I saw the watchtowers with their searchlights, I couldn't keep myself from shuddering. My memories of barbed wire and armed guards in Auschwitz were much too raw.

When we first arrived at the shores of Cyprus, there were trucks waiting to take us to the internment camps. We were driven though a tall gate. When I strained my eyes in the darkness, I could see the bulking shapes of dozens of tents dotted about the compound. We were ordered to leave our knapsacks and handbags behind so we could be showered and disinfected.

SISTERS IN THE STORM

I found myself shaking convulsively. I remembered the stories of Chelmno, when the people hung their belongings neatly on hooks so they could get them back after they showered, and then they stepped into the shower rooms and were met with a stream of poisonous gas. The British won't do that, I tried to tell myself. They won't. They wouldn't, they couldn't, they'd never.

A touch on my arm snapped me out of it. Sarah was looking at me with a sad smile on her lips. I knew she understood what I was feeling.

People were being divided up and directed to various tents, but Sarah and I managed to stay together. We came to a long table where we were registered, and taken aside for a quick medical examination. Then we were directed into a separate section of the tent. Our clothing and bodies were sprayed with a foul-smelling disinfecting liquid that dried into an irritating powder. The whole procedure was frustratingly drawn out and time-consuming. It was hours before we were finally finished. We were given back our knapsacks and told to enter the enclosure that would let us into the camp.

The line proceeded very slowly. We were passing through a narrow corridor of wire, and there was not very much room to move. There was only enough room for two people to walk next to each other, and I couldn't shake the feeling that I was walking in a cage. We shuffled forward, trying to make out the faint silhouettes of people standing on the other side of the wire. I realized that they must be Jews who were already interned in the camps. I wondered if I would meet anyone that I knew.

Suddenly, I heard a hoarse voice cry out, "Is there anyone here from Lodz? Lodz? Anyone from Lodz?"

I gave a convulsive start. I hadn't even heard the name of

my hometown mentioned since I left Poland! Throughout all my travels, most of the refugees I had met were from other countries—Hungary, Yugoslavia, Romania, Austria and Czechoslovakia. Whom did I know from Lodz? My childhood home had disappeared during the war. We had gone from a happy, united home in Lodz to an anonymous number in Auschwitz. Even our return to Lodz was not a return to our hometown. The place had changed into a strange, alien city that I didn't recognize. And now I heard someone asking for Lodz. Could it possibly be someone from the old Lodz I remembered and loved so well?

"Is there anyone here from Lodz?" the question was repeated.

I had drawn abreast to the small group of people standing on the other side of the fence. It was one of the young men of the group who was asking the question.

"I'm from Lodz!" I shouted. The momentum of the line was already carrying me away. I tried to push back, but it was impossible. I turned my head and shouted again. "Yes, we're from Lodz! We were in Lodz!"

It was too late. Whoever it was who had called out, he was already a dozen feet behind me.

We finally reached the end of the enclosure and entered the "Summer Camp" of Cyprus. The "Summer Camp" consisted mostly of singles, with a few couples; the "Winter Camp," at the other end of the island, was made up mostly of married couples and young children.

When we entered the "Summer Camp," we were surprised to see that most of the people there seemed to be our own age. There were a dozen camps dotted about the enclosure. Our Agudah group filled up Camp 60 and Camp 61. Sarah and I were directed to a tent in Camp 60. We

285

entered an army-green tent which was empty except for a small table and a kerosene lamp hanging from the center pole of the tent. This was to be our home for the coming months.

As we stood surveying the stark emptiness of our tent, two young men knocked on the tent flap and came inside. Only one of them was bearded. The clean-shaven one was carrying a pot of tea, and the aroma was enough to remind me of how terribly thirsty I was feeling.

The young man carrying the pot handed it to me with a smile. "You're from Lodz?" he asked. "Tell me, what is your name?"

I accepted the pot of tea gratefully, feeling a little embarrassed. "You wouldn't know me," I said. "My name is Landman." I handed the pot of tea to Sarah, gesturing to her to take a drink. I knew she was thirstier than I was.

"Landman, you say?" The bearded young man looked at me intently. "Your father was Reuven Yosef?"

"Why, yes," I said, staring at him with astonishment.

"Binyamin was your brother?"

"Yes," I said softly. The thought of Binyamin was still hard to bear. Still, I was perplexed by how well this young man seemed to know my family. Who was he?

"My name is Korzetz," the bearded young man said. He tipped his head to the side, waiting to see if I would show any recognition of his name.

"Leibel Korzetz?" I asked with disbelief.

The Korzetz family had been good friends of my parents. This man standing in front of me looked exactly like the man who had been my father's *chavrusa* in the summer, when the Korzetz family had rented the bungalow next to ours. But who looked the same as they had in the years before the war?

The young man shook his head. "Leibel Korzetz was my father," he said quietly. "I am Chananiah, his son."

I slowly lowered my knapsack to the ground. Chananiah Korzetz had brought a flood of happy memories rushing back into my mind, memories of the happy days in Lodz before the war. I didn't know whether or not to be grateful to him for it.

He began to pepper me with questions. "Did your father survive the war? What happened to Binyamin? Maybe you saw my mother in Auschwitz?" I answered his questions to the best of my ability.

In the meantime, his clean-shaven young companion stood listening quietly without saying anything, until finally he suggested that I drink the tea before it got cold. The two of them thanked us politely and left.

Soon afterwards, the other girls sharing the tent with Sarah and me came inside. There were seven of us altogether. Two were Bais Yaakov teachers, and I was delighted to know I would have someone to help me nearby. The two girls, Rosa Fleisher and Martha Reish, would be able to teach me and help me keep the *mitzvos* and follow *halachah*.

Unfortunately, they only gave us six cots. The seven of us stood surveying the situation. Almost every single one of us offered to sleep on the floor for the night, until we could arrange for another army cot to be brought into the tent. Before anyone bedded down on the ground, however, a childhood friend of mine walked into the tent with a big smile.

"Rivkah Gocial!" I shrieked as I flung my arms around her neck. "How did you know I was here?"

She hugged me back. "I heard that a ship arrived from Romania," she grinned. "I knew you had been to Bucharest, so I figured you were probably on board." Seeing that we were short a cot for the night, she invited me to sleep in her tent, where there was extra room. The problem was solved for the night, and we got our extra cot in the tent on the following morning.

Life in Cyprus was a fascinating study of conflicting emotions. Frustration—we knew that we were forced to wait until the British allowed us to enter Eretz Yisrael. Anticipation—the British would eventually let us in. It was only a matter of waiting. Discomfort—the section of Cyprus where we were encamped was a miserable one. Fulfillment—the Agudah had set up an efficient network of learning and *frumkeit* in Cyprus, and we were able to make efficient use of our time. I spent a year in Cyprus, and I ran the entire gamut of emotions during that short period of time.

Our camp was situated in a very sandy area. The place was barren of anything green—no grass, trees, flowers or bushes. Sometimes, there were sandstorms so violent that one could not walk outside for fear of being blinded. During the fall and winter, the rain would drum frantically against the tents, and we would end up slogging ankle-deep through tenacious mud. I kept several cans under my cot so I could prop them up in strategic places when the rain leaked into the tent.

It was obvious that the British were determined to make our lives miserable. Actually, it almost made sense. The British knew there were hundreds of idealistic young men who wanted to join the fledgling army in Palestine. Throughout my entire stay in Cyprus, a clandestine training program went on, and dozens of young men were smuggled out of the enclosure and into Eretz Yisrael. There were also *frum* boys who participated in that operation, and no *frum* girls at all.

Food and water were a problem in Cyprus. The British supplied us with a bare minimum. Food was supplemented by a canteen installed by the Jewish Joint Committee, where food and other basic items were sold for a very low price. Unfortunately, some of us didn't even have enough money to spend a few pennies on food. Things were made even more difficult for the delegates from Eretz Yisrael who had come to Cyprus illegally in order to help us. They had no food allotted to them at all, and they would have had nothing to eat if not for an ingenious plan that was carried out with every ship that came into Cyprus. When the British asked for a list of the people on board, the leaders of the ship would supply several fictitious names of non-existent people. These names, dubbed *neshamos,* were adopted by the delegates from Eretz Yisrael. They would use the names of the *neshamos* to claim the food they needed.

Water was supplied to us every second day. A large truck would arrive bearing a huge tank of water, and everyone grabbed a can and ran, pushing and shoving, to get into line. Sometimes, I ended up waiting in line for hours to get my precious can of water.

Although we were crowded and uncomfortable, the Agudah provided us with lots of food for thought. When the Cyprus prison camps had been established in 1946, several groups came to help organize assistance for the inmates. The Sochnut *shlichim* and the Mazkirut-Meshutefet groups from the *yishuv* were interested in collecting data from us and instituting their policies. They also recruited several young men and trained them before smuggling them out of camp and into Eretz Yisrael to join the army. The Agudah, how-ever, was primarily interested in organizing our lives accord-ing to Torah and *halachah.*

The first thing they did was set up a rabbinate to administer marriages. The rabbinate had its hands full with this task; there were many second marriages, and tremendous research was needed to discover whether or not a husband or wife who had disappeared during the war was really dead. Eyewitnesses were needed, but they were almost impossible to find. A committee was set up to check the credibility of the witnesses, since many people were inclined to give false information in mistaken sympathy for the *agunah*.

The rabbinate also arranged to have a section of the beach roped off to serve as a *mikveh* for the married ladies. No one was allowed to get married, not even the non-religious couples, without a certificate stating that the woman had been to the *mikveh* before the wedding.

The Agudah set up steady learning periods for boys of all ages. One shipload of boys that had arrived on the ship *Arba Charuyot* was led by a forty-year-old man named Leibel Kutner, who called them his "children." They had their own *beis medrash* where they learned, *davened* and ate together. Every available moment was spent in making up for the years they had lost during the war.

The Agudah arranged *shiurim* for the girls, too. They organized seminars, held lectures, established schools on elementary and high school levels and taught nursing and other skills to those who were interested. Our lessons included Hebrew, *Pirkei Avos* and the geography of Eretz Yisrael.

My roommates, Martha Reish and Rosa Fleisher, were a tremendous help to me in my lessons. They also managed to get a sewing machine for us, and we were able to repair our tattered clothing. Most of my clothes at this point were made of tent canvas that we had cannibalized.

One thing Cyprus did for us was help cement lasting friendships. The littlest thing was enough to bring two girls together. I remember watching one heavily pregnant young woman come into the camp, looking worried and anxious. I asked her what was troubling her, and she explained that she didn't know how to get a message to her parents, who were already safe in Eretz Yisrael. I ran back to my tent and came back with an envelope and stamp. She was speechless and overjoyed. The young woman never forgot it; it was such a little thing, but it made all the difference in the world.

# CHAPTER 39

■

# Matchmaking

ARLY ONE MORNING, A WEEK OR SO AFTER WE HAD arrived in Cyprus, I was wandering through the camp and watching people doing various tasks. Since the tents were little more than inadequate shelter from the rain and wind, everyone did everything outside on long tables. I was near the tent of Leibel Kutner's "children," and I stopped to watch one particular young man who caught my attention.

He was the same clean-shaven boy who had come with Chananiah Korzetz to my tent on my first night in camp. He was cleaning a suit, which surprised me. Most people were living in canvas, and those who owned clothing didn't bother keeping it clean and neat. This boy, however, seemed to care about his appearance. I was further impressed when I saw him shining his shoes a few days later. Polished shoes lasted about five minutes or so in the sand, but this boy was polishing his shoes anyway. I remembered something Binyamin had once told me about a *yeshivah bachur* keeping a neat appearance in order to make a *kiddush Hashem*. I became more and more curious about this boy who seemed so different from the rest of the group.

A few weeks later, I ran across my old friend Miriam, who had been in Halbstadt with me. She had married one of the boys from our transport, and they were one of the only couples in our camp. We were sitting together on my narrow cot, reminiscing about our life in Zagreb and Bucharest, comparing it with life in Cyprus. She mentioned that her husband Elchanan had many friends among the boys who had arrived on other ships. I sat up abruptly, wondering if she could satisfy my curiosity.

"I noticed that there's one boy going in and out of your tent a lot," I said with studied casualness. "Who is he? He's always wearing a suit, and I never see him without a *Gemara* under his arm."

Miriam gave me a sharp look. "Chanka, do you like him?"

"Like him?" I sputtered. "Who said anything about liking him? I just asked who he is, that's all."

Miriam eyed me with amusement. "His name is Avigdor Eilenberg. Maybe you know his family, Chanka. He's from Lodz. He's a very nice man from a good family. He's very close with Elchanan." Then the conversation turned to other topics, and she seemed to forget about my question.

The next morning, Elchanan came over to me and asked if I would be interested in meeting one of his friends. I was taken aback and more than a little dismayed. Meet a boy? Me? I'm still young, I'm not ready for that kind of thing! Then I heard my voice saying, "Well, it depends on who it is."

Elchanan rocked on his heels, his hands behind his back. He was looking somewhere three inches over my head as he spoke. "He's one of Leibel Kutner's boys. If you want to see him, I'll be walking with him to the *shul* tent for *Minchah*." He turned around and walked away.

It was ten o'clock in the morning, and *Minchah* was hours away. I was in an agony of suspense, wondering which boy Elchanan had in mind. Maybe, just maybe, it would be the boy who had brought me tea.

The hours dragged by slowly, until finally it was time for *Minchah*. I found a strategic position where I would see Elchanan no matter what direction he came from. I went through a few frantic minutes when I was sure that I had missed them, when suddenly I saw Elchanan just entering the *shul* tent. The boy walking with him was indeed Avigdor Eilenberg. I swallowed hard before turning and bolting back into my tent.

The next morning, Elchanan knocked on my tent flap and asked for an answer. Falteringly, I agreed to meet the young man. Elchanan merely nodded and went off. He came back later, telling me to wait outside at five o'clock in the afternoon.

I was nervous and embarrassed as I went out to meet him. I had never met a young man before with serious intent in mind. What would I do if he expected me to be bright and witty? Would I know what to say?

As it turned out, he didn't give me a chance to say anything at all. After we had greeted each other, he started telling me about his *yichus*. I listened dumbly, feeling my spirits sink down to my shoes.

When I came back to the tent, Sarah was waiting to

pounce on me. "*Nu*, how did it go? What happened? Did you like him? What did you say?"

I sank down wearily on my cot. "Nothing's going to happen," I said, depressed. "All he did was talk about his *yichus*. He's related to Rav Kalish, the Chief Rabbi in Bnei Brak, and he's the eighth generation from Reb Dovid'l Lelever, and he's related to the Skierniewicer Rebbe, and we spoke about *chassidim* the whole time, and I don't think it's going anywhere."

"Maybe he was nervous," suggested Sarah. "You know, a lot of people babble like that when they're nervous or embarrassed." She gave me a sly smile. "Besides, it seems to me that you paid an awful lot of attention to what he was saying."

I blushed. "Well, the only *yichus* we have is the Rema."

Sarah burst out laughing. I grinned sheepishly, realizing how ridiculous it sounded. Still, I was resigned to the thought that he probably wouldn't be interested in seeing me again.

I was very surprised when Elchanan came over to me the next morning and told me that Avigdor was interested in seeing me again. I was determined to be a good conversationalist this time, and I began by describing my father and grandfather.

He smiled at me and said, "I knew your father and grandfather. In fact, I was even in your house once." As I stared at him in astonishment, he went on to describe my parents' home in complete and accurate detail. Suddenly, it dawned on me where I had seen him before.

"Did you learn by Baruch Gelbard, right next to Bilander's bungalow?" I asked.

When he nodded, I relaxed. He was a secure piece of my past, and I began to feel more comfortable with him. The rest of our meeting was easy and congenial, and I looked forward to seeing him again.

At our third meeting, Avigdor asked me the question. I answered, "Yes," and I was engaged.

I went back to the tent that night in a daze. It was Thursday, and I woke up the next morning with a feeling of unreality. I washed my skirt and blouse for *Shabbos,* just like any other Friday. As I was hanging my things out to dry, Avigdor came over and told me that he had made arrangements for a *lechayim* that night after the *seudah* to celebrate our engagement. I nodded, smiled, walked carefully back into our tent and threw myself onto my cot, crying hysterically.

Poor Sarah looked at me askance. "What's wrong, Chanka? What is it? What can I do to help?"

I shook my head helplessly, tears still streaming down my face.

"Are you having second thoughts?" she asked worriedly.

"No, of course not," I sobbed.

"So why are you crying?" She threw up her hands in frustration.

"I don't know," I sniffled, sitting up on the cot.

"Listen," she said with exasperation in her voice. "Do you care about Avigdor?"

I couldn't help being amused to get this pep talk from my little sister. "Yes, very much," I answered seriously.

"Then stop crying, and be happy that you found your *zivug!*"

I burst out laughing. I wondered briefly if being engaged meant having such violent mood swings, but for the moment, it didn't matter. I hugged Sarah tightly, happy to have at least one member of the family together with me for my *simchah.*

After our beautiful *lechayim* that night, Avigdor and I saw each other often. He used to bring me a small bowl of farina every morning, which I shared with Sarah. Sometimes he would get me some sugar, which I ate up as quickly as possible, to the amusement of my friends. It seemed that my body was lacking in sugar due to the malnutrition I had suffered during the war, and the sugar he brought me came in very handy.

We had been engaged for two months when the boys from Avigdor's ship were given permission to leave for Eretz Yisrael. Avigdor promised to stay in touch, and I watched forlornly as the people of the *Arba Charuyot* ship pulled out of the harbor. The inmates of Cyprus were processed according to ship, and I knew I would have to wait along with the rest of the passengers of the *Knesset Yisrael* before I would be able to rejoin my *chassan*.

When Avigdor arrived in Eretz Yisrael, he made his way to Bnei Brak and settled in with his cousin, Rav Kalish. He managed to send me two pounds sterling, which was the equivalent of two month's salary in Cyprus. However, he had to save money for an apartment for us in Eretz Yisrael; we needed "under-the-table" money as well as money for rent, furniture, bedding, dishes and cutlery. Jobs were nonexistent, and Avigdor was scraping together whatever he could.

During the ten months of our separation, I went to as many weddings in Cyprus as possible. Sarah laughed at me, telling me that I could hardly "take notes" for a normal wedding at a Cyprus one.

She had a point, of course; Cyprus *chasunos* were anything but normal. Friends had to take the place of the *kallah's* mother. There was no difficulty in renting a wedding hall, since the *chupah* took place in a tent. Nobody got officially invited to a wedding; if you knew the *chassan* or *kallah*, you came and danced and ate the simple food that was put out for the wedding *seudah*.

*Brissim*, too, were very happy occasions. Everyone used to crowd into the tent, holding their breaths until they heard the thin wail announcing that the *bris* had taken place. Then they all burst out into loud chatter and laughter, sharing in the *simchah* of the happy parents.

I, too, joined in the festivities, looking forward to the time when I myself would, *im yirtzeh Hashem*, be making a *bris* for my own future sons.

# CHAPTER 40

---

## So Near, Yet So Far

A YEAR PASSED IN CYPRUS. DEPRESSING AS IT WAS TO BE banned from Eretz Yisrael, we had our learning and friends to help pass the time, as well as a high dose of adventure. There was the time when the *yeshivah* boys got high on *Purim* and made several disparaging remarks about the inferiority of the women. Two girls took matters into their own hands and sneaked over to the boys' tent that night. When we awakened the next morning, we discovered that the boys' tent had collapsed into a heap—all of the ropes fastened to the tent pegs had been cut. The boys never found out who had sabotaged the tent, but even they had to admit that it was good *Purim shtick*.

Of course, there were also the occasional demonstrations staged by some of the more enthusiastic boys in camp. I'll never forget the sight of torches hurling through the air at the British soldiers, forcing the soldiers to run for their lives. Most of the time, however, the British stayed away from the compound, and we were able to go about our lives in peace.

I found myself drawn to the children's camp, where young children's lives were slowly put back together. Perhaps I was so interested in this because of my work for the Agudah in Bucharest. I volunteered to be of assistance, and I became very close with one young girl named Syma Pajman, who was living as a Jewish girl for the very first time on the island of Cyprus.

Syma had been only five years old when her family fled the Germans. They hid for some time in a forest, cowering among the trees during the day and begging for food from gentile farmers at night. None of the farmers gave them any shelter. Some gave them a little bit of food, but most chased them away and set the dogs on them. Her younger brother and sister, twins only seven months old, were literally starving. In the end, her mother abandoned the twins on the doorstep of a home, hoping that someone would be kind enough to take them in.

Finally, an old gentile woman agreed to keep Syma in hiding. At first, she kept her hidden in the cellar. Later on, the old woman passed Syma off as her relative from a distant village. Syma was slowly but surely poisoned against the Jews; the woman constantly told her horror stories about Jews drinking the blood of innocent Christian children. She became accustomed to going to church every Sunday, and by the end of the war, it was almost impossible to tell she had ever been a Jew.

Several months after the war ended, Syma was in the pasture with the old woman's cows when she was approached by two men. She recognized one of them as her father's brother, and he began to talk to her in Yiddish.

Syma was terrified. She streaked back to the old woman's house, screaming on the top of her lungs, "Jews came to kill me! Jews came to kill me!" The old woman promised her that she would make sure the "evil" Jews would not be able to touch her.

Syma's uncle, who had followed her back to the house to see where she lived, showed up on the old woman's doorstep several days later, flanked by two Russian soldiers. He told the old woman in no uncertain terms that he was taking his niece with him. The old woman looked nervously at the soldiers standing next to him, and she didn't put up any argument at all.

Syma, on the other hand, kicked and screamed, refusing to leave the old woman's side. It took several minutes before she could be persuaded to go with her uncle. Finally, she stopped crying and agreed to go with him.

Little Syma was taken to Germany, where she joined a small group of Jews waiting for a transport to Eretz Yisrael. Her ship suffered the same fate as mine, and she ended up in Cyprus. There, under the loving tutelage of the Bais Yaakov teachers, Syma began a new life among Jews.

I took Syma under my wing, telling her stories and keeping her happy. I was sorry to leave her behind when our turn finally came to leave the island of Cyprus and go to Eretz Yisrael.

Much as I regretted leaving Syma behind, I was ecstatic to be on the final leg of my journey. I had travelled through Europe, sailed on a rickety ship, been arrested and sent to Cyprus, and now I was actually on my way to my final destination!

We boarded the ship, shivering with excitement. We were free, really free, and almost home!

Then reality intruded. The British still weren't ready to let us go. We were interned in Atlit, a quarantine camp where we would be forced to stay for a three month period.

It's 1947, I thought bitterly. Is this freedom or a concentration camp? Why am I surrounded by a tall wire fence? It was as if the British were telling us, "Listen, we didn't ask you to survive. You insisted on living, but we don't have to make it easy for you."

But at least we were in Eretz Yisrael itself. Our journey was over, and we were standing on holy soil. Still, it was crushing to know that we had yet another wait before the British would let us go free.

Atlit was one gigantic prison with separate quarters for men and women. Even married couples were only allowed to see each other during the day. The British did not let us forget that we were prisoners under surveillance. We impatiently counted every day that passed, for each day brought us that much closer to freedom.

When we first arrived in Atlit, we were led through a tall wire gate to an area of white hot sand and wooden barracks. We were fenced in by wire fences, and the fences were lined by faces pressed against the wire. These were people who had reached Eretz Yisrael earlier, and now they were anxiously looking for any sign of relatives or friends. Desperate to find familiar faces, these people would come down to Atlit every time they heard that another ship had come in. Scanning the myriad faces, I wondered if Avigdor had heard about the arrival of our ship. Would he be waiting for me? I had no one else in Eretz Yisrael, no relatives who would be waiting for me and helping to expedite my departure from Atlit.

The air rang with the shouts and calls. People, straining to catch a glimpse of the inmates coming into Atlit, would cry out the name of a person they thought they recognized, only to be disappointed when the person turned out to be a stranger who bore a faint resemblance to the person they were seeking. Here and there, one could see a joyous reunion, but for the most part, the faces along the fence were filled with disappointment.

Then I stopped, and my mouth dropped open. I couldn't believe it. It wasn't possible! I stared across the compound at her face. Her mouth moved, but I couldn't hear a sound. Hashem, please, let this be real! Don't let this be a dream!

I raced over to the fence, our hands touching through the wire mesh. It was Aunt Bluma, my dear aunt whom I had last seen in the death camp of Auschwitz. She was here, she was alive, she was well! We tried to kiss each other through the fence. It was awkward, but I didn't care. She had tears streaming down her face, and so did I. I was overwhelmed to know that another member of my family had escaped Europe and survived the war.

I turned around and shrieked Sarah's name on the top of my lungs. She, too, came running, and the same happy scene repeated itself. I turned away slightly, wanting to give Sarah and Aunt Bluma at least a modicum of privacy, and found myself looking straight at a tall, handsome man standing right next to Aunt Bluma. He was staring directly at me, and he made me feel very uncomfortable. Who was this man that dared to intrude upon our joyous reunion?

As I stared back at him, he silently pulled a handkerchief out of his pocket and handed it to me. Still staring, I took the handkerchief mechanically and used it to wipe my eyes. Aunt Bluma gave a little shake and then laughed. Apologizing for not doing so earlier, she proudly introduced us to her husband. I blinked. This man was her husband? What happened to my Uncle David? Then I remembered. David had died of disease in the Lodz ghetto. Aunt Bluma must have remarried.

My new uncle seemed to be a very efficient man. He walked away from the fence, only to come back a few minutes later to tell us he had received permission from a guard for the two of us to come over to their side for a few minutes. Sarah and I excitedly followed the two of them into a small hut where Aunt Bluma was staying.

As we sat down on the bed, Aunt Bluma started to pepper us with questions. Had we heard anything about Tatteshe? Had we seen him since Auschwitz? Had we heard anything at all?

We had to disappoint her. We all knew that if Tatteshe was still alive, we would have heard from him by now. As gently as possible, we broke the news that he had probably been killed in Auschwitz. Aunt Bluma just sat there, her mouth stretched in a stiff, frozen smile. The last hope for her brother was gone.

Suddenly, she got up, mumbled an "excuse me" and rushed out of the little hut. We sat there helplessly, miserable at the knowledge of how much we had just hurt her by telling her the truth.

Our new uncle sat regarding us for a few moments. Then he stood up abruptly and walked over to the linen closet. He rummaged through the towels for a few moments, then he pulled out a picture and handed it to me together with a white envelope.

"Chanka," he said in a pleading tone. "Please take this picture. Have pity! Don't let her ever see it again."

I looked at the picture for a long moment, and I had to hold back my tears. It was a picture of my two little cousins, Aliza and Rivkah. In the picture, Aliza was five and Rivkah was three. They looked absolutely adorable, dressed in identical outfits with big black bows in their hair. As I sat there, staring numbly at the picture, my uncle quietly explained.

"It seems that when the picture was originally made, Bluma sent it to a relative in London. The relative sent it to us a few months ago, and the first time Bluma saw it, she went into shock. She had to be hospitalized for several days." He sighed heavily. "She's completely obsessed with the picture, and she gets very upset every time she looks at it. Chanka, please hide this picture so that your aunt should never see it again."

I carefully put the picture into the white envelope and slid it into my pocket. My heart went out to poor Aunt Bluma. I remembered that horrible day of the *shpero*, when Aliza and Rivkah had been taken out of the hospital and hurled onto trucks by the Nazis. Aunt Bluma had run frantically after the trucks, hearing the frightened cries of her daughters, wailing, "Save us, Mommy, save us!"

She had almost reached the truck when a German soldier grabbed her by the arm and smashed her to the ground, stunning her momentarily. By the time she stumbled to her feet, the truck was gone. I understood why her husband didn't want her to have the picture. It was too raw and painful for her.

When Aunt Bluma returned, she seemed to have composed herself. She didn't ask us any more questions about Tatteshe or the family. Instead, she talked about how she had met her new husband in Italy after the war. She chattered about her own trip to Eretz Yisrael, telling us about the hardships and complications she had gone through. Sarah and I nodded with complete understanding. After the last two years, it all seemed very familiar.

Suddenly, she stood up. "There's something I want to show you," she said.

She walked over to the linen closet. I held my breath as she stuck her hand underneath the towels, feeling around for the picture.

"Where is it?" she muttered to herself.

Then she shrugged and came back to sit down again.

"I must have misplaced it," she said brightly. "Some other time, perhaps."

I steeled myself to show no reaction. I breathed a silent prayer that the conversation would turn to something else.

But Aunt Bluma said nothing. She sat down next to me, holding my hand and playing absently with my fingers as she stared at nothing in particular. An awful silence dragged itself out. No one seemed to know what to say.

Ten long minutes passed before tears began to trickle down her cheeks.

"Did you know, Chanka," she said in a tremulous voice, "that you are sitting next to a murderer?"

I gave a convulsive start and began to stammer a protest.

"Oh, no, Chanka, don't argue with me! I know what I'm

saying. I am a mother who murdered her own two little babies. I know that I did it, and nobody will ever convince me otherwise."

She lifted her chin and turned away. I sat there helplessly, wishing I could think of something to say. Aunt Bluma blamed herself for putting her children in the hospital when they were so desperately ill, and then failing to die together with them in the crematorium. She considered herself a murderer because she did not manage to save them during the *shpero*. I couldn't bear the thought of how much pain she was putting herself through every day by blaming herself for her children's death.

Aunt Bluma never mentioned the missing picture to me again. In later years, however, after Avigdor and I had settled into our apartment in Bnei Brak, she sometimes came to visit me. Almost every time she came, she found an excuse to rearrange my closets. I had a ground floor apartment, and I used to have a vegetable garden. Once, when I was busy weeding my garden, I glanced through the window and saw Aunt Bluma looking in my linen closet. She was carefully shaking out each piece of linen, unfolding it completely before putting it back. I stood up and watched silently as she went through all my drawers. She opened up every single envelope she found and unfolded every piece of paper. I started to cry. I knew she was looking for the picture of her two lost children.

# EPILOGUE

———————————————— ■ ————————————————

WO DAYS AFTER MY RELEASE FROM THE PRISON CAMP of Atlit, I settled into the Mosad Sarah Schenirer in Bnei Brak. Pesya Sherushevski, who was a graduate of Sarah Schenirer's seminary in Cracow, had established this home for religious girls without a place to stay. I grew very close to Pesya during the months I stayed in the home before Avigdor and I were married; she was a wonderful person, warm and giving.

In addition to being our "home," the Mosad Sarah Schenirer was also a teaching institute. There were regular classes with Pesya and our *madrichah*, as well as optional counseling sessions given by Pesya. I never missed a single one of those sessions; Pesya was a true teacher, able to inspire us all.

The usual topic of Pesya's sessions was "Ethical Behavior in Daily Life." Pesya often used Tyla Rynder, the girl who had saved so many lives in Auschwitz, as the perfect model of ethical behavior. Pesya spoke clearly and concisely, painting a distinct picture of how a true *bas Yisrael* should behave. Our values, which had become twisted and skewed in the upheaval of the previous several years, gradually regained a more even keel.

With the loving care of Pesya, who fulfilled the dual roles of devoted mother and stern father, I slowly healed.

Six months after my arrival, Avigdor and I were married at the Mosad. Together, we were ready to begin a new life.

Sarah, who had grown into a beautiful young woman, was married two years later. Her husband was the son of Mrs. Rivkah Weiser, one of the few courageous women in Auschwitz who had risked her life to light candles for *Shabbos*. She, too, had her entire life ahead of her, ready to begin anew.

Who can tell the future? In 1930, when Hitler's party had little political power, did anyone imagine that six million Jews would be dead within fifteen years? In 1944, when Sarah and I stood in line before the gas chambers, waiting our turn to be gassed to death, did I ever expect to be living peacefully together with my husband in Eretz Yisrael? There is no such thing as security, and there is never reason for utter despair. Only Hashem knows what is going to happen to us. Instead of wondering about what is going to happen next, let us remember our past and understand the lessons of our history. Let us work towards bettering ourselves, so that we may be *zocheh* to see the coming of *Mashiach, bimherah viyamenu, amen!*

*My father as a young man.*

*My grandfather at my grandmother's graveside.*

אלטא תחואלא לערנער

אשתו חשובה וצנועה
קשיטה צדקה גמלה
יראת ה' רבנית לב
הנכברה מרת
אלטא תחואלא
אשת ר' אלוזן אהרן
הנפטר
ב ר' יצחק אלכסנדרא...
נפ' בת כ"ו שנה
ר' אייר תרצ"ג
ת נ צ ב ה

*Avigdor and my oldest son Yossi*

*My sister and I at my wedding.*

*My sister is to my left.*
*The picture on the wall is of my father.*

# GLOSSARY

**agunah:** woman unable to obtain a *get*
**aishes chayil:** woman of valor
**Aktion:** round up [German]
**Alteste:** supervision [German]
**ani maamin be'emunah sheleimah:** I fully believe
**appell:** roll call [German]
**bachur(im):** boy(s)
**bar-mitzvah:** *halachic* adulthood
**baruch Hashem:** Blessed is the Name; thank Heaven
**batei medrashim:** study halls
**beis medrash:** study hall
**bekeshe:** *chassidic* festive garb
**bitachon:** trust
**biur tefillah:** explanation of the prayers
**blokowa:** block warden
**brachah:** blessing
**bris:** covenant
**chaburah:** group
**chacham:** wise person
**challos:** *Shabbos* loaves
**Chanukah menorah:** candelabra for the Festival of Lights

**chassan:** bridegroom
**chassidim:** adherents to *chassidus*
**chasunah:** wedding
**chavrusa:** study partner
**cheder:** elementary Torah school
**chinuch:** training
**chodesh:** month
**Chumash:** Book of the Pentateuch
**chuppah:** bridal canopy
**daven:** pray
**Elul:** Jewish month, roughly corresponding to September
**emunah:** faith
**Eretz Yisrael:** Israel
**frum:** observant [Yiddish]
**gabbai:** synagogue president
**gedolim:** great ones
**Gemara:** part of the Talmud
**gemillas chassadim:** acts of kindness
**goy(im):** gentile(s)
**haggadah:** liturgy for *Pesach seder*
**halachah:** Jewish law
**Hallel:** special prayer of praise

315

**Hashem:** the Name, G-d
**hashkafos:** views
**hasmadah:** diligence
**Havdalah:** concluding ritual of *Shabbos*
**im yirtzeh Hashem:** if G-d wills it
**Judenrein:** free of Jews [German]
**Kaddish:** mourner's prayer
**kallah:** bride
**kapo:** inmate guard [German]
**karpas:** part of *pesach*
**kavanah:** concentration
**kedoshim:** martyrs
**kedushah:** holiness
**kehillah:** community
**kibbutz:** group
**kiddush Hashem:** sanctification of the Name
**Kiddush:** sanctification of *Shabbos* or festivals
**kittel:** traditional white garment
**lekavod Yom Tov:** in honor of the festival
**lechayim:** to life, traditional toast
**Leshanah habaah b'Yerushalayim:** next year in Jerusalem
**limudei kodesh:** sacred studies

**Maariv:** evening prayers
**maasim:** deeds
**maggid:** preacher
**Mammeshe:** mommy
**marranos:** secret Jews [Spanish]
**marror:** bitter herbs
**Mashiach:** the Messiah
**masmid:** diligent one
**matzah:** unleavened braed
**mazel:** fortune
**mein kind:** my child
**mentchlichkeit:** common decency
**mesechte:** tractate
**mezuzos:** scrolls affixed to the doorpost
**midos:** character traits
**mikveh:** ritual bath
**Minchah:** afternoon service
**minhagim:** customs
**minyan:** quorum of ten
**Mishnayos:** part of the Talmud
**mitzvah:** Torah commandment
**Motzei Shabbos:** night after the *Shabbos*
**muselman:** zombie
**navi(nevium):** prophet(s)
**nefesh:** spirit
**neshamos:** souls
**niggunim:** tunes
**parnassah:** sustenance

316

**parshah:** portion of the Torah

**parshas hashavua:** weekly Torah portion

**pasuk:** verse

**perek:** chapter

**Pesach:** Passover, early spring festival

**peyos:** earlocks

**pikuach nefesh:** a matter of life and death

**Pirkei Avos:** Chapters of the Fathers, Talmudic ethical tractate

**Purim:** Festival of Lots

**rabbanim:** rabbis

**revere:** camp hospital [German]

**Ribono Shel Olam:** Master of the Universe

**Rosh Chodesh:** New Month

**Rosh Hashanah:** New Year

**seder(im):** Passover feast(s)

**sefer(im):** book(s)

**seudah:** feast

**seudah shelishis:** third *Shabbos* meal

**Shabbos:** the Sabbath

**Shacharis:** morning prayers

**Shema Yisrael:** Hear, O Israel

**shidduch:** match

**Shir Hamaalos:** part of *Tehillim*

**shiur(im):** lecture(s)

**shiva:** seven day period of mourning

**shlepping:** procrastinating; dragging [Yiddish]

**shlichim:** agents

**shtiebel:** *chassidic* attitude

**shul:** synagogue [Yiddish]

**Shulchan Aruch:** Code of Jewish Law

**siddur:** prayer book

**Sifrei Torah:** Torah scrolls

**simchah:** rejoicing

**sofer:** scribe

**tallis(im):** prayer shawl(s)

**talmid:** pupil

**Tatteshe:** daddy

**tefillah:** prayer

**tefillin:** phylacteries

**tefillos:** prayers

**Tehillim:** Book of Psalms

**Torah:** the complete body of Jewish teachings

**tov:** good

**treif:** not kosher

**tzaddik:** righteous man

**tzaddikim:** righteous people

**tzaddekes:** righteous women

**Vidui:** declaration of transgression; confession

**yeshivah:** Torah school

**yeshivah bachur:** *yeshivah* student

**yichus:** pedigree

317

**Yiddishkeit:** Jewishness
**yiras shamayim:** fear of G-d
**yishuv:** settlement
**Yom Kippur:** Day of Atonement
**Yom Tov:** festival

**zchus:** privilege; merit
**zemiros:** songs
**zivug:** preordained match
**zlotys:** Polish money
**zocheh:** worthy